WALKING WONDERS

Stepping Your Way to a More Creative Life

Enjoy your own –

WALKING WONDERS!

Stepping Your Way to a More Creative Life

CATHLYNN RICHARD DODSON

Best,
Cute
Romancing the
Past B&B
Oct. 2009

iPUBLISH.com
at Time Warner Books

For information address iPublish.com, 135 West 50th Street, New York, NY 10020.

 An AOL Time Warner Company

ISBN 0-7595-5019-0

First edition: July 2001

Visit our Web site at www.iPublish.com

Contents

Contents   vii

Introduction

The practical benefits of a daily walk are unquestionable. The National Sporting Goods Association ranks walking as the number one fitness sport, ahead of swimming, biking, and aerobics. Millions of Americans participate in "exercise walking." In the twenty-first century, however, walking is evolving into something even better. Physicians agree that walking can be beneficial in providing a sense of calm to its practitioners. James M. Rippe, M.D., author of *Fit Over Forty* (William Morrow), says that "forty minutes of walking at any speed will help reduce stress." *Healthy Living Magazine* reports that "during exercise, the brain relies more on the creative right side and less on the rigid left side, so new thought processes may be an inherent part of movement." Well-known experts in the fields of self-help and creativity such as Julia Cameron, Sark, and Jon Kabat-Zinn tout walking as a meditative and creativity-enhancing activity. Writer Brenda Ueland, a prolific writer in the 1930s, had this to say of walking: "I will tell you what I learned myself. For me a long, five- or six-mile walk helps. And one must go alone and every day."

As a writer, I'm intrigued by the creative and meditative possibilities of walking. My own discovery of walking as a tool to enhance my creative potential came about somewhat by accident. For the past several years, I've used Sarah Ban Breathnach's *Simple Abundance* as a daily meditative guide. Having a good meditation or "thought for the day" to read before my daily walk was very important to me. It set the tone for reflection and spiritual connection as well as opened me to my deepest level of awareness. Later as I walked, however, I noticed that while at first I tended to reflect on the reading, at some point my mind began to relax and turn to exploring the beauty of the world around me. Somewhere in that process, I'd start to find metaphors for my writing in what I saw. Something inside me opened up and I made the connections between words and images—I knew what I needed to say and how I needed to say it. I could go home, and the words would flow. This became such a valuable tool for me, I began to use it every day.

In addition, I discovered that walking enhanced my life in general. Things I saw in nature became metaphors for events that were happening in my life and these were magically translated into solutions for problems. Walking, I decided, provided an excellent source of therapy, a creative boost, and great exercise—all free and available at any time!

While my daily reading of *Simple Abundance* provided some wonderful essays for thought and reflection, the more I walked the more I found myself wishing these meditations would help me in exploring the metaphors available to me in nature. As a result, I began as I walked to collect "ideas" for such a book. *Walking Wonders: Stepping Your Way to a More Creative Life* is the compilation of my ideas, explorations, discoveries.

Paying close attention to the world around you during daily walks not only increases your awareness of the deep beauty and interesting elements of nature, but also provides a myriad of metaphors and examples for life in general. If you walk in conjunction with reading this book, you will improve your powers of observation, and you'll also be able to incorporate greater productivity and creativity into any aspect of your life and find solutions to problems where you never thought of looking for them before. You'll awaken inner resources you never knew you possessed.

First, however, it's necessary to change how you observe the world. Most of us don't take time to "stop to smell the roses"; half the time we don't even see them because our minds are too full of the mental chatter we carry with us through our days. In her book *Wanderlust: A History of Walking*, Rebecca Solnit says that while walking, "the mind, body, and the world are aligned, as though they were three characters finally in conversation together, three notes suddenly making a chord. Walking . . . frees us to think without being wholly lost in our thoughts." *Walking Wonders* helps create new patterns of discovery. Opening ourselves on a regular basis to the world of nature allows us to use and develop innate tools we all possess—inspiration, focus, discipline, and reflection—to discover deeper self-awareness. These tools are vital to any creative process and are referred to again and again in the essays in this book.

Walking Wonders offers each person opportunities to explore and define his or her own creative potential. Too many self-help books tell you what you should and shouldn't do rather than encouraging you to search for authenticity, meaning, and balance in a personal way. The book may be a companion, but the journey is yours alone. Each of us has inherent artistry and talent; it's just a question of discovering it for ourselves. In *Walking Wonders*, you'll find explorations to guide your walks, but the discoveries you make will be yours alone.

Beginning Your Personal Explorations

There are no right or wrong answers and no right or wrong ways to proceed with your explorations. You may want to use a journal, a notebook, or even your PDA to write down observations, experiences, and metaphors that may come to you on your walks. After a few excursions, you'll know what note-taking method works best for you. You can read my essays either before your walk or after. If you read them afterward, then you may want to consider whether you found any similarities between your experience and mine. You may discover that you and I are walking completely different paths in more ways than the obvious. If you prefer more guidance beforehand, then you may want to read the essays first and use them as food for thought during your walk. At some point, you may want to write about your own experiences and discoveries, thus creating your own collection of "walking wonders."

Twelve explorations and essays are provided for each season: spring, summer, fall, and winter. Each essay relates to an area of life in which you may need or want to develop a deeper understanding. Remember to use the creative tools mentioned earlier during your meanderings: inspiration, focus, discipline, and reflection. They are an important part of any creative endeavor you decide to undertake. *Inspiration* motivates and provides the courage to begin new projects and endeavors of all sorts, from jobs to relationships. In this world of so many distractions, *focus* is necessary if we're ever to accomplish anything. *Discipline* sounds worse than it is—it means that you've got to be willing to commit to and work at the things you want to accomplish. *Reflection* asks that you look beyond the surface not only to understand how your past has played a part in who you are today, but also to discover what's really important to you. During my walks, I've used each of these tools at one time or another to find solutions to everything from problems with novel plotting to personal crisis. I hope the same becomes true for you.

Because we all lead full and hectic lives, the book's organization allows you to work at a pace compatible with your lifestyle, whether you happen to be a sporadic walker or a daily one. You can go straight through the explorations in order (perhaps choosing to work on one each week), or select a subject that is appealing to you or well-suited to the weather or climate in your part of the country. Perhaps you'll want to mix and match the essays in different sections, allowing you to find unique and different discoveries on each and every one of your explorations.

Because it's so difficult to keep our lives in balance, *Walking Wonders* hopes to assist you in accomplishing this overwhelming goal by grouping together several of your "I wish I had time to's." Use the short meditation to provide a moment of solitude and quiet; consider your walk as both daily exercise and time to reflect and become more aware of both nature and your inner self; let your own essay be your creative outlet for the day. As you begin to incorporate inspiration, focus, discipline, and reflection into your walks and your life, you'll find you've discovered a magic button that gives you peace and perspective.

I encourage you to let this book be a tool, no matter what your talent, occupation, or interest. Each one of us has a creative side; we may use it in the world of business or education or homemaking or art. As you begin to develop your powers of observation and refine your instinctive understanding about those observations, you'll discover new ways to solve problems, a deeper understanding of yourself, and a greater appreciation for life's abundance.

Walking Wonderfully

There's also a wonderful by-product of using this program: by walking on a regular basis, you'll also be stepping your way to good health. Don't worry too much about form and fitness, but you may want to keep in mind that it's important to have a good pair of walking shoes, and to fill your strides with purpose and energy. I suggest spending a few quiet moments reading and reflecting on the exploration before beginning your walk. Consider putting your whole body into each movement. Be aware of your body, but also be aware of the world around you. Allow your body to carry you, but give your mind the freedom to watch and wonder. Be open to what the world has to offer you on each new day. The object of these explorations is to encourage you to make your own unexpected discoveries, to let your daily walking meditations take a direction that's different from what you expected. That's perfectly all right. Nature may have a particular lesson it wants to share. Let instinct be your guide. Be awake. Be open. Be there. Best of luck on your journey!

Autumn to winter, winter to spring,
Spring into summer, summer into fall—
So rolls the changing year, and so we change;
Motion so swift, we know not that we move.

—Dinah Mulock Craik

The Wonders of Walking
Spring Explorations

Spring is a time when the world opens up and says "Look at me—aren't I splendid!" The explorations of spring should inspire and awaken you to the potential and possibilities in your own life. Don't be surprised if you discover that all the magnificence of a beautiful spring day rests deep inside you and is simply awaiting its wake-up call. A wonderful walk may provide a gentle reminder that a new day has dawned and it's time to let all that you are out into its warming light.

As you walk and begin to take a closer look at spring, think about the feelings that this season awakens in you. Are you filled with energy and enthusiasm? Does that vitality tend to ripen as you move toward the full days of summer? If so, use this energy now as you begin your journeying and journaling. Open the deepest part of yourself not just to the refreshing sights of spring, but also to the colors, scents, and sounds—this season brings its own special graces to the world. Trust me, spring will bring you a new message and experience every day if you stay tuned in to its gifts.

Today, take a moment to revel in this season of life. Let spring encourage you to explore and bring to life the creativity that lives inside. Find your own new beginnings; excavate sensations and memories long locked away in your heart and ask what messages they're offering you now; rediscover your wilder nature and your individuality. Have fun with spring and watch your life bloom.

Exploring New Beginnings

It's spring—trees and flowers bursting like variegated sunlit firecrackers. What do they remind you of? How would a writer describe the colors of spring to someone who can't see them? How might an artist paint those same colors? How does this season make you feel, knowing the trees will bud every year, no matter what? As you walk, think about your own feelings about birth and renewal. Does spring inspire you to find new ways to bud in your life? Do these feelings spill over into your creativity? What would you like to begin in this season of new beginnings? Read "New Beginnings," then write about your own.

New Beginnings

My favorite thing is to go where I've never been.
—Diane Arbus

Renewal seems to fill the air during spring. As I was walking today, thinking about my writing, I almost tossed out the idea of writing about renewal because it seemed so common. However, as I strolled along streets accented with new life, taking in the light feeling of hope in the air, noticing the tiny buds of green just beginning to shoot forth from the trees and shrubs, bulbs about to burst into blossoms of color, hearing the cheery dialogue of carefree birds, I realized there's no denying the absolute truth of it: spring is all those things. Even more, spring speaks of promise.

Life, like the seasons, goes round and round, but somewhere in the depths of our being, we keep the promise of spring. The bulbs that we plant in the fall, scraggly brown and apparently void of anything resembling life, choose this season to burst forth with the yellow of daffodils, the red of tulips, and the pink and purple of hyacinth. Birds build cozy nests from lifeless twigs and twine, in treetops and tiny houses, where soon their speckled eggs will crack and twitter with new life. Lawns that have slept blanketed in brown begin to glow with the green of spring. In the midst of the deepest winter of our souls, we too hold to the hope of renewal, an inner knowing that life is simply resting till the wakeup call of spring comes with color and vitality.

When I ventured out into the world today, noting it reclothing itself in green, I realized that once again I, too, had a chance to start over. I could go home, shed the trappings of winter, clean my house and soul of whatever holds me back and keeps me from moving into the lightness of life, full of joy and a sense of possibility. Spring grants me this time of cleansing, this permission to re-create, yet I can also grant it to myself, by bringing forth my own spring when life seems to have been too long and cold a winter.

As I walked past bulbs blooming, baby birds twittering, and lawns smiling with life, I asked myself what had been lying dormant in my life. What ideas, projects, experiences had slept the winter away in my heart and now longed to burst forth with their own new life? By the time I rounded the corner of my street, my count was up to ten. A writing project I'd been putting off, a trip out of town to see a friend I hadn't seen in some time, a shopping excursion for a couple of bright outfits to fill up the empty space I would make when I cleaned the closet.

But oddly enough, like the dormant bulbs of the daffodils, I knew there were other, deeper calls anxious to come to life this season: expanding my writing into an area where I'd been afraid to venture, exploring a career option I'd been hesitant to move toward, deepening the bonds of my relationships with those closest to me. Spring's awakenings lie both on the surface of our world and lives, and deeper. I knew as I picked up my pace that it would ultimately be those deeper longings that added the most color to my life.

Today, as the world around me wakes from its winter slumbers, I too am ready to wake up and begin again.

Exploring Positive Outlook

Pay particular attention to the birds as you walk today. In particular, find a bird that likes to sing. Where does this bird perch as it serenades the world? What kind of bird did you find? What does its song remind you of? Have you ever noticed a bird singing in this particular place before? What do you think this bird was singing about? What does the song say to you personally? Does the melody inspire you? Birds seem to find their own particular brand of happiness at any given moment. Birds always seem to take a positive outlook on life. Do you bring this kind of joy and hope to the work you do on a daily basis? What does your song sound like? Read "Bird on a Wire" and think about how you might bring a joyful attitude to your own routine.

Bird on a Wire

Hope is a thing with feathers
that perches in the soul,
And sings the tune without the words
And never stops at all.

—Emily Dickinson

Some days are made for singing. There's a spring in my step, lightness in my heart, and I feel I could trill and twitter like a songbird from dusk to dawn. But singing like that every day—I don't think so. There are plenty of days when singing is the last thing I want to do. Days when the writing isn't going well and I'm convinced I'll never sell a thing. Days when hope seems lost somewhere in the endless blue sky. On those days, I don't even want to hear a song on the radio!

Which makes me wonder about the sanity of the mockingbird who meets me on my walk at Chelsea and Medford—same time, same place, every single day. I'll give him credit: the song is always a bit different. This guy's got a repertoire that would make Tony Bennett jealous. He makes the phrase "happy as a lark" seem lackluster. But he's a bird, and I can't help wondering what exactly he's got to be so happy about.

Still, as I continue my meander, I guess I can see a few things that might make me want to sing if I were a bird. The freshness of the morning, the sun in the sky, the air I breathe, life—isn't that enough? Sometimes I get so caught up in worrying about where I'm going and how much I'm going to accomplish, I forget to be happy about the little things that greet me on a daily basis. I forget the "simple abundance," as Sarah Ban Breathnach calls it, that lives all around me every single day. I lose my hope and my way, and most of all, my song.

The mockingbird reminds me to take note of the two squirrels vying for first go at the feeder in that yard across the way. He calls to my attention the sparrow family teaching junior how to fly, quivering wings and all. He announces the arrival of the lilies and the budding of the crepe myrtles. He celebrates everything every single day; every instant is filled with hope for him.

In my own life, isn't there so much more to be joyful about than just the simple abundance of the world of nature? There's my home, and my family, my friends, my cats, time to spend at work I enjoy, tea in the mornings and a glass of wine on the deck in the afternoon—all this, and more, more, more.

Mr. Mockingbird chirps and chimes and fills his lungs to bursting with the joy and hope of each new day. How he inspires me to be happy about all that I have in life, and all that I can be! He also reminds me to enjoy the journey, take joy in the daily work, something I seem to be forgetting lately. In fact, this cheery little reminder makes me think I need to get some music of my own going once I'm back at my desk, to remind myself that with a song and a positive outlook, joy and hope can be my constant companions, just like they're his.

The abundance I'm given on a daily basis inspires me to sing a song of joy and hope as I walk and work.

Exploring Scents and Sensuality

Find a sweet scent on your walk, something that titillates your memory to an almost forgotten passion. Where does the scent come from? A pretty flower, or a tree or shrub? What memory do the scent and the scene evoke, what feelings does the memory awaken in you? Do sweet scents bring heightened sensuality to your walk? To your life? When was the last time you felt sensual in your life? Not necessarily in a sexual way, but a time when you felt all your senses were awake and participating in whatever you happened to be doing? What can you do to have such an experience today? Are you able to capture that sensuality in your writing or other creative work? Read "A Bride's Passion," then think back to your favorite sensual experiences.

A Bride's Passion

Smell is a potent wizard that transports us across thousands of miles and all the years we have lived.
        —Helen Keller

There's a shrub that blooms here in the South in the late spring and early summer that's commonly known as "bridal wreath." It has long slender limbs, dark green foliage, and tiny sweet white flowers—simply inhaling the scent of bridal wreath reminds me of new love: fresh, green, sweet, innocent. The place where anyone who's ever been married started out. Remember?

I remember long passionate kisses and the smell of my lover that I couldn't seem to get enough of. I remember being entwined with his long slender limbs as we made love that seemed to go on endlessly. I remember the newness of the relationship, the things we'd never shared before and the things we happily discovered we had in common. Sensual days of innocence and trust, the belief that he was everything, and together we could do anything. Yes, I do remember . . .

Unfortunately, many of us lose that closeness even before the first year is over. We seem to have forgotten the "coming back year after year" part. Not so with the bridal wreath—it's there, every year, and I'm always eager for its heady passionate fragrance, for those sensual memories.

In life, all too soon we forget the passion and the "sweet" times, in relationships both with others and with ourselves. We forget to take time for the sensual, to take time to share those moments of heightened awareness. As brides we become "queens" for a day, but what about the other 364 days of the year? The groom may soon forget he married a queen, but the queen forgets it, too. When was the last time you treated yourself like someone special? Taking time to put yourself first just takes too much time.

Nature's advice would happily tell us all is not lost. There must be spaces in love, just as there are in the seasons. Our bridal wreath can't bloom year-round, and even if it did, we'd become so accustomed to its fragrance that probably we wouldn't even notice it. No, it fades away and we must wait until another season for its return. But we can take its memory with us, and seek other sweet scents of passion throughout the year. We can look for ways to bring sensual memories to the creative work we do. Perhaps a drop of essential oil on a light bulb or a scented candle might help evoke a memory of a certain time or place. A walk through a fragrant garden may bring to life a moment of love and passion. Maybe it's necessary to live with the ebbs and flows of emotion, but look around carefully—there are ways to experience sensuality, the fulfillment of our senses, each and every day.

Today, I'll look for ways to re-awaken sensuality in all that I do.

Exploring Heart

Look at the homes around your neighborhood. What are they like? Do they speak of wealth and stressful living, or family and happy times? What do you think the people who live inside might be like? Do you think they are cold or warm, happy or negative? What about the house itself gives you these impressions? How can you tell if a house has "heart"? What ideas do the homes you see awaken in your creative "heart"? Do you see anything in these houses that inspires you to create fictional stories about the people and their lives? Now read "Beauty and Heart" and then write some reflections of your own about places with heart.

Beauty and Heart

God's love is taking place in front of our eyes.
—Eknath Easwaran

One of my most enjoyable walking pastimes is to study the houses on my route. Even though I often see the same places day after day, I never tire of wondering about the people who live inside and what their lives are like. I have an unproved theory that you can tell a lot about people by looking at their house and yard. Maybe this theory stems from my need to create a "story" around what I see, thus allowing the exterior to be the door into that realm of make-believe.

When I look at homes and the yards that keep them company, I guess what I'm really looking for is beauty and heart. What I've decided is that even though the exterior of someone's property is overrun with plants and appears unkempt, the yard itself will always have heart, whereas the home itself may be in question. The yard, you see, has the heart of God in it, no matter what its caretaker does or doesn't do to make it appear lovely on the surface. Why does a yard have heart? Because as Eknath Easwaran tells us in his book *Your Life Is Your Message*, the fact that trees give us the air and food we need to live is God's way of expressing love. "God doesn't say 'Here, open this envelope. There are some coupons inside. You can go and buy love wherever it is available.'" No indeed. Trees take our carbon dioxide and freely give us back oxygen. Nature, by its very essence, is full of heart.

A home, on the other hand, must have its heart provided by the people who live inside. Creating beauty is one thing. With a little effort and imagination, anyone can bring lovely design and furnishings into the home—a touch of warm color on the walls, friendly and comfortable furniture, beautiful accessories. But heart, heart is a different matter entirely. There's really no way to tell from the outside if a home has heart. Heart is the give and take, the love and surrender, the people who support and care for each other. A home can look magazine-cover exquisite but if it doesn't have heart, it's not a place you really want to be.

Once I had a friend whose home had all the trappings of comfort and beauty, but the more time I spent there, the more I noticed its lack of heart. When I visited this place I was always taken with its charm, but I never felt safe. Eventually time proved my inner discomfort correct and the friend and I went our separate ways. I still miss the loveliness of her home, but I don't miss the out-of-balance relationship I had with its owner.

Even with writing, it's important that the work be more than just a superficial look at a topic. Fancy words and creative metaphors don't mean anything if the writing itself lacks heart. If I'm writing for the wrong reasons, my work won't have the depth needed to carry it deep inside the hearts of others.

Walking, working, or seeing with the heart creates balance. Give and take. Nature does it so easily. Why can't we?

Today, I'll consider ways in which I can bring heart into my own home and creative efforts.

Exploring Coexistence

Find a trumpet vine, morning glory, or honeysuckle vine (or some other vine common to your area). Describe the vine. Talk about its strengths and weaknesses. What animals like vines? Which ones don't? Do you have any vines in your own life? What are they? Are they holding you back from accomplishing your goals? Why is it important (for creative types especially) to learn to coexist with both the beauty of the flowers and the chaos of the weeds? Read "Entwined in Vines" and think about how this might apply to your own creative life.

Entwined in Vines

Not out but through.

—Aniela Jaffe

Funny, honeysuckle never seems dangerous in the spring. Neither does trumpet vine or morning glory or Carolina jessemine. When I left the house this morning, I couldn't help but think how lucky I am to have that arbor with those beautiful yellow blooms of Carolina jessemine. Along the road, the honeysuckle smelled so sweet and delicate that I had to stop for a few minutes and suck the nectar from a few flowers. The hummingbirds seem to think the same thing about the trumpet vine on my neighbor's west wall. These dainty scented blossoms decorate a spring day like jewelry on an elegant woman. What would a fine spring morning be without them!

Today, however, I notice that my neighbor has chopped down the trumpet vine that stretched across her outside wall like fine lace. For a moment I think, "What a shame!" and I feel for the stray hummer that missed its chance for a succulent feast. And I wonder why anyone would commit such a travesty. But then I know, and the pictures my mind paints are especially pretty ones.

Those vines grow deep underground. They harbor all kinds of unwanted pests and clog up the plumbing lines. They wreak havoc on the foundation. They knock down fences. They twist and cling and cause nothing but trouble. Or so I've heard.

Personally, I wonder if there's a way to coexist with vines. Isn't it only when people let them get out of control that the problems occur? What if we kept them trimmed back, so that they could bloom all they wanted in the spring but they didn't do their miscellaneous dirty deeds during the rest of the year?

I know that sometimes it's necessary to trim back the vines in my own life, to make sure what blossomed yesterday hasn't become a burden today. When I trim my vines and prune my life of what's gotten out of control and chaotic, I know it frees me to focus on what keeps me blooming and happy. As a writer, I know that trimming my work often makes it clearer.

On the other hand, maybe it's best if certain vines are left to grow in the wild, out in the woods or on trees in the park, so the plumbing stays happy and so do the birds. Maybe sometimes we try to tame what's wild and chaotic instead of leaving it where it can have free run of the land. Maybe that chaos is a necessary part of my creative nature. When I need to write about the tangles and the untamed, I need to know it's there to tap into.

Everything has its time and place. Shadows and light, wild and tamed—artists need both.

There's a time and place for all things, be it weeding the vines in the garden or appreciating the beauty they bring.

Exploring Overload

What pushes the "overload" button in your life? How do you deal with overload when it happens? Does walking help? How does walking affect overload when it's happening? Are there any aspects of this season that cause you to feel overload in a physical way? What are they? Read "Overload" then write about your own experiences with this issue.

Overload

Walking allows us to be in our bodies and in the world without being made busy by them.
—Rebecca Solnit

April showers have indeed brought May flowers—finally! At last the fading gloom of winter has turned to vibrant green. I've found myself diving into a million activities both inside and out—cleaning the attic, repainting the planters, making sure my home is ready for whatever lies in the days ahead.

I realize as I begin my walk that I've neglected myself lately. I haven't really taken time to stop and enjoy my morning tea—or to take my daily walk. It's so nice to be out now, seeing everything gloriously in bloom.

As I turn the corner, I discover a real feast for my eyes. The shrub that was barely budding a week or two ago is now a sunburst of yellow—Lady Banks roses in full spectacle! Rarely do I get this treat—Lady Banks is a floribunda that, like old roses, blooms only once every year. With boughs hanging heavy with tiny yellow flowers from tip to stem, she's a virtual bouquet of light, beaming proudly as I stop to run my hand across her delightful golden glow.

Rounding the next corner, I notice another display of the lady's vanity, this time spreading high up two nearby trees—trees now devoid of life, swallowed by the overload of yellow roses weighing down their branches. Beautiful, but sad.

This overload of yellow makes me recognize that lately I've been allowing myself to get a little too weighted down with work and cleaning and even creating. All that activity seems to have blinded me to the fact that I need to take some time for myself. It's wonderful to feel so energetic and enthused, but all that energy isn't going to last forever. How much longer until I'm bent and broken like those trees on the corner?

I slow my pace a little, determined to take plenty of time to enjoy my walk today. Breathing deeply, I allow the magic of this lovely spring day to refresh and renew me. I let my thoughts drift to what I might do to better take care of myself today and in the days ahead, so that I can avoid overload completely. More time over tea and reflection in the mornings, an afternoon nap, maybe even a trip to the ice cream shop for a special treat. Definitely another five minutes admiring Lady Banks!

Today I will take time to renew myself, knowing that overload is bringing me a message: "Take care."

Exploring Guidance

If you look carefully as you walk, you may begin to notice that birds are pretty family-oriented. What do you see them doing to help each other? Do birds make good parents? In what way? How is bird parenting similar to people parenting? Would you make a good parent—to a bird or a person? Why or why not? What kinds of guidance do parents need to offer children today? How can birds inspire people to be better parents? In your creative life, where do you look for guidance? Do you offer guidance to those not as far along in their creative work? Read "Flight Training" and think about creative ways to show guidance to others in your own life.

Flight Training

I think the lesson I have learned is that there is no substitute for paying attention.

—Diane Sawyer

Lots of new parents are out there right now. It's an exciting time to be walking! Every kind of bird from the most ordinary sparrow to the brightest bluejay to the most dignified red cardinal seems to have new offspring to take care of. I'm amazed by the efficiency and concern birds seem to have for their little ones. For instance, did you know that most bird parents continue to feed their young by mouth long after they've left the nest? Did you know you can spot a "juvenile" bird by the way its wings quiver—and by the way mom or dad hovers protectively while it is still taking flight training?

In a world where so many children are lost and going astray, we might take a lesson here. Our children desperately need this kind of loving guidance before they're set loose to make their mark on the world. Too many of us have turned them over to the TV to guide and nurture them, forgetting that what they really need is just a little time and attention from mom and dad. Indeed, parenting itself can be a form of artistry.

Eknath Easwaran, founder of the Blue Mountain Center of Meditation and author of *Your Life Is Your Message*, recommends learning to "put other people first—beginning within the circle of your family and friends, where there is already a basis of love on which to build." Building a loving family takes the same kind of creative energy that any other artistic endeavor requires. You might even consider modeling your own actions on other parents you most admire.

Of course, we parents may have other goals and dreams beyond parenting that we want to accomplish as well, but how long does it take to give a child a daily hug and tell them you love them? What do we teach our children by withholding something so simple? How would our world be different if each parent saw the care of his or her children as a form of artistry?

And if you don't have children of your own, perhaps you can find another way to offer such love and guidance to a child in need. The world is full of children craving a parent's love—if you could bring that love into even one life, you'd be doing the world a great service. Doing so will reward the creative soul in ways you never imagined.

Today, I'll give a child a smile and a hug. And I'll give the birds a little prayer of thanks.

Exploring Flow

Pick a day with lots of clouds. As you walk, note the different kinds of shapes. How would you describe them? Do you see any familiar sights in the clouds—like a balloon or a face? What particular images do you see? If you were a cloud, where would you go? What would you do? How do you let flow be a part of your life and your creative pursuits? Now read "Bows and Flows" before writing about your own experience of "flow."

Bows and Flows

When love and skill work together, expect a masterpiece.
—John Ruskin

Some days there are masterpieces in the clouds—have you noticed? Today I was looking for a masterpiece, but it was such a bright blue open sky day I didn't have much to work with. I was reminded of those canvases you see at modern art galleries that are painted in one color and considered to be great art. Not that color isn't wonderful, but where is the art in covering a canvas with a single color?

It wasn't entirely a wash, however—no pun intended. Some slight evidence of white provided just enough inspiration for me to ponder. Little ribbons of white, streaks like a chalk on pavement, reminded me that although they weren't in attendance today, the bows and flows probably weren't far behind. In fact, looking out the window right now, I can see them already beginning to gather. Ribbons blow in first, I guess, and the bows come a bit later.

Bows and flows: that's clouds in a nutshell. Today the ribbon and now the bows remind me that this world is just one big gift, wrapped up and ready to surprise us. Some of the surprises are pleasant ones, bringing joys and thrills that make birthdays out of ordinary days. Others aren't so pleasant, but that's where the flow part comes in. When we unwrap a gift from a loved one that's not exactly what we had in mind (or worse!), normally we put on a smile and go with it, not wanting to hurt or offend the giver. What I realized today is that we've got to learn to flow with life like that. Go with the gift: it may hold unexpected insights.

In life we fight the gift, we get mad about what's being dished out to us, we feel sorry for ourselves, become victims to what potentially holds the precious. Instead, we might try giving ourselves up to the moment, the walk, the event, and see where it leads and what gift it has to offer.

Like today, when I looked up and saw that ribbon, I had no idea it would lead me here. I felt a little disappointed there weren't more masterpieces in the sky, waiting to be explored. Instead, there was a grander gift—I just had to stop and "go with the flow."

Today, when I pull the ribbon to release the bow, I promise myself I'll let the flow of the gift take me where I'm meant to go.

Exploring Fresh Perspectives

Are there any newly painted houses in your neighborhood? What does the smell of fresh paint remind you of—something from your past, or something you want to accomplish in the present? How does it make you feel to see a house with a fresh coat of paint? Are there any areas of your life that need a fresh coat of paint? Maybe you need a fresh perspective on a particular project you're working on. If so, how might you find a different way of looking at it? Read "Fresh Paint," then write about some things you'd like to begin seeing from a fresh perspective.

Fresh Paint

You create your life with each choice you make.
—Stephen C. Paul

I took a new route today and came upon a house getting spiffed up with a fresh coat of paint. The pungent odor wafted through the air, letting me know something was up even before I actually came upon the house. A couple of men in paint-splattered white slapped brushes thick with a reddish-brown color on the trim. The house had been around more than a few years—things were definitely looking up for it. I wondered how it felt to be that old house, getting that fresh coat of paint. Would the paint lift it to a new place, making it feel like it was somehow new again?

Would the people inside see the world differently, now that their home wore this fresh coat of confidence?

Not long ago I bought a new car. Actually, it wasn't really a new car—it was a 1995 model. Still, I noticed something interesting as I drove the car: I felt new. I felt as if something bright and fresh had been wrapped around me, elevating me to a level I wasn't functioning on before. It was a wonderful feeling, maybe like getting a fresh coat of paint.

For me, that's exactly what spring does every year: it wraps me and my world in a fresh coat of paint so that everything feels fresh and new and better than it did before. During this time of year, I find that just taking my walk every day gives me a fresh perspective on my life. That perspective may apply to a problem in a relationship, something I've wanted to accomplish but haven't known how to proceed with, or some difficulty I'm having with my writing. It's as if I've been given a "happy pill" that makes me suddenly see everything differently. It's like an instant spa treatment. Some folks pay thousands of dollars for mud baths and herbal wraps; I'll take a mile's worth of spring any day—it's free!

I'm so grateful for the wonderful freshness spring brings to my life, making me feel renewed and alive and ready for another round!

Exploring Memories

Does your neighborhood have any parks with picnic tables and swings? If not, you might try to find a walk where there is a park. Reflect on what part parks have played in your own life, past and present. Where does thinking about parks lead your thoughts today? Does walking by or around a park spark any creative ideas for you, or does it awaken memories about your own past experiences that you'd like to write about? Read "Pastimes," then write some of your own memories of park experiences.

Pastimes

Writers live twice.

—Natalie Goldberg

Sometimes walking leads me away from the future, into the past. It never happens consciously, and perhaps it happens most often when I'm working on a story of my own that takes place in a different time period. Maybe at those times I'm more receptive to being led through a door into yesterdays. Sometimes when I follow that road I can almost imagine I'm living in a time long gone, different, yet the same.

I love to hear stories about my neighborhood from old-timers who've lived there all their lives, some whose families have been there for generations. One seventy-five-year-old friend told me recently that his mother used to ride her bicycle to the lake at a nearby park. I could just see his mother—wearing a dress and bonnet—riding her bicycle along the dirt road that was surely treeless back then, pedaling her way with a blanket and library book in the basket. The "park" would probably have been a pond with a gravel path leading down to the water; the paved walkways and children's playground didn't exist in those days.

The park I know today not only has paved paths and playground equipment, there are picnic tables with covered pavilions, ducks in the pond who may or may not be transplants, parking lots, and people in jogging shorts that would have made my friend's mother blush. The pond itself is lined with layers of trash, and the noise on the playground makes concentrating on a novel difficult. Besides, who reads outside anymore? We've gotten too used to air-conditioned comfort these days to have any idea what reading on a blanket by the lake might be like. Not to mention the fact that nobody bicycles anywhere either; driving one's car to take an "exercise" walk is more the norm.

For just an instant though, if I stop and close my eyes, I can see and hear it the way it was all those yesterdays ago: the quiet broken only by an occasional bird chorus, a few people here and there stretched out on blankets in white linen suits, children playing with homemade boats near the water. I smell the aroma of popcorn; the vendor might even have a little organ and a playful monkey. A group of geese squawk, arguing over a handful of bread someone has tossed their way. I like going back there, remembering a different, simpler life. I like feeling that I'm a part of something that stretches on and on.

Still, the memories aren't always so very far away. The geese still fight over the bread tossed out by walkers and their children; the children still love to play with boats near the water; there are even a few couples stretched out on the grass—snuggling more than reading, though.

When I return to my desk, I find I'm able to carry some of those wisps of memory back with me, enhancing not only my day but my writing as well. Times have changed, but not always as much as we might think. Something of the old lingers on with the new, and that's nice to know.

The past is only a memory away, and today, for an instant, I'll capture a memory and bring it to life once more.

Exploring Unexpected Images

Can you spot a tree that doesn't look like a tree? What does it look like? Do you see an object, or a person, or something else when you look at it? How would you look if you were a tree? What might it feel like? Are you firmly rooted like a tree in your life? Do you want to be? How can you carry unexpected images into your creative work? How can you use them to discover unexpected things about yourself? Read "The Woman in the Tree" and then write your own reflection about trees you saw on your walk today.

The Woman in the Tree

Look for a long time at what pleases you, and longer still at what pains you.
—Colette

Her branches reach like arms toward an empty sky; her trunk etched in the anguish of a barren cry . . .

Many years ago, my husband gave me a wonderful poem by Anne Morrow Lindbergh that compared a tree to the stages of a woman's life. The previous lines aren't from that poem, though, but rather my own attempt at poetry after noticing a particular tree on my walk today—a long slender sycamore, reaching out with arms pleading, begging for a grasp at life, but coming up empty time and time again. The tree made me remember Lindbergh's poem, and I came home and read it again, remembering the stages through which we women must pass before finally coming to a place of wholeness.

We do come to wholeness eventually, I believe, but the journey is often a long arduous one, and the woman I saw in the tree today was still struggling to embrace the kind of life she wanted for herself. Seeing her made me sad, for I'm at such a place in my life, trying to break free of any bonds that might hold me back, yet often coming up empty-handed as I reach out to grasp the fullness of life.

Still, the woman in the tree wasn't ready to give up yet. She stood tall, not yet bent by trial or pain, making me pause to wonder how tall I will stand in the years to come. Will life bend my branches with its hardships or will I find myself ever ready—eager even—to grasp for the sky? I hope the poems and stories and books I write in the coming years explore the same kind of wonder at living that Anne Lindbergh maintained in her writings, in spite of the pains she met in her own life. Some day, I hope my words reach out like slender branches to touch others as hers have touched me.

The woman in the tree today spoke to me of frustration, but she also spoke to me of hope. I'm glad I looked at the tree long enough to see both.

Today I'll try to remember that behind every moment of frustration lies the kernel of hope necessary to help me see my way forward.

Exploring Your Wilder Side

Go on a nature walk. You'll want to try to find a wild area for this walk. What makes it wild? How is it different from your usual walking location? Do you have any wild spaces inside of you? What are they encouraging you to do that your grown-up self is forbidding? How can you explore the wild side of your writing or other creative projects? Do you avoid such explorations? Why is it important to let this part of yourself "out" from time to time? Read "Wild Spaces" then reflect on how wildness affects your creativity.

Wild Spaces

All women's boundaries are crossed at one time or another
and they are crossed continually.
— Elizabeth Winthrop

The path has boundaries, but the wild space does not. Today, I take the way of the wild, because my own boundaries seem diffused and confused.

A nature preserve backs up to the area where I live, and I rarely go there alone; it's not advisable in this day and age for women to go wandering around wild spaces without a dog or a man or at least a can of Mace. I can't help myself, however. I need the uneven dirt paths, the misshapen trees and the weeds grown taller than I am. I need to allow myself to flow into that open space and feel my pain. In my real world,

I've learned to contain it like milk in a carton, and today it needs to spill out and sink into the dry, receptive earth.

The wild space gives me permission to spill, to flow, to feel. Things are protected and safe here. Feral cats have taken up residence inside hollow tree trunks, and in some spots, I feel certain feral people have done the same. There's evidence of living in the wild space, but it's not the kind of living I'm accustomed to, nor is it something I'm very open to exploring in my writing. I find I hold my boundaries close, and getting beneath the surface to my wild depths isn't always an easy thing for me to do.

Along one path, I see the remnants of a community of homeless people, a city built of logs and old tires and stray bricks and cement girders. Rings where fires have been laid make me wonder what these people speak of in the evenings, as they draw near the flames. Do they share stories, or speak of families and times past? Does the word "boundary" truly no longer have meaning for them? Will that day ever come for me? Has it come already, even there in the safe harbor of my green and yellow kitchen, where I hold back the wild urgings of my soul?

Nothing hurts me in the wild space, and I see no one as I walk the paths where others have gone before. I let the tears spill out, willing an answer to the concerns in my heart. Two mockingbirds dart past me, their calls loud and angry, their own emotion echoing through the day. People, birds, animals come to this space, returning to a place where nature unites and makes everything once more its own. The trees bend close and protect us from whatever would do us harm; the grasses listen as we share our sorrows. The sun dries our tears; finally, I, at least, can go back, and face the world of boundaries once more. Perhaps, however, in facing this world, I've discovered a slender crack I'll be able to slide into back at my desk, an entry into my own wild world.

I'm thankful there are still wild spaces in this world, where we can go to be free and protected from the hurts of life.

The Wonders of Walking

Summer Explorations

Summer is a time for slowing down and focusing on the fullness of the world around you. Now that spring has inspired you with the potentials and possibilities of life, you need to "pull focus," as they say in the movies, and get centered on what you really want to accomplish. How do you feel as you enter the season of summer? Do you feel ripe and expectant with the excitement of what lies ahead? If so, you can use this energy to keep yourself enthused and in touch with what you want out of this particular time in life.

Open yourself to the slow wonder of summer. Take a moment today to think about summers past. How did they shape and influence you? Remember those splendid summers when you were young, filled with the laughter and timelessness that only youth knows. Remember how once the summer had passed you always felt as if you'd grown into a new person. How would you like the summers of your future to shape your life? Would you like to recapture that sense of time standing still? If so, maybe you can try to do it during one of your walking explorations.

Summer is a time of fullness of spirit. As this summer progresses, let that fullness spill into your own life and keep it focused and abundant. Try to remember, however, to slow down a bit and just enjoy those long languorous days. Spend some time enjoying the conversation of birds, thinking about ways you might want to do some repotting in your life, and reveling in the full bloom of summer's glory. Become a child again, and let summer carry you gently through its timeless hours.

Exploring Beauty

Early summer is a perfect time to experience the full rich beauty of nature. On your daily walks, you'll probably see an abundance of flowers in full bloom, relishing the warmth of the not-yet-too-hot sunshine, brightening the yards of many of your neighbors' homes. Notice the many varieties of flowers as you walk and pay special attention to those that draw you. Is it the color that appeals to you, or the ways they look, or perhaps the scent? What feelings does a particular flower bring to mind? Do you have pleasant memories about certain types of flowers? Read "In Full Bloom," then, as you walk today, make notes for your own thoughts about flowers.

In Full Bloom

Beauty is eternity gazing at itself in a mirror.
—Kahlil Gibran

It's early summer, and there's nothing I'd rather do than stop and smell the roses. Actually, I enjoy just looking at them, and all the other amazing gems in the garden as well. Spring wakes them up, but in early summer flowers are at the height of their glory. Summer is a time for taking special walks, and one of my favorites is a little retreat in Fort Worth called Fuller Garden. Though it's named for someone who contributed to the garden society, the name is apt right now—Fuller has never been fuller.

This isn't a strenuous walk, more like a ramble through a picturesque wonderland, but I enjoy strolling along its paths from time to time, imagining myself on a vacation to some faraway place rather than almost in my own backyard. When I'm in a garden like Fuller, I could be anywhere, at any time; it's almost as if time has indeed stopped and I've just settled into a pleasant moment of eternity. So most days all I want to do is simply enjoy the moment, soak up the fullness of its beauty and try to take a little portion of it back into the real world with me.

Fuller Garden has a little bit of everything a garden should have. When you first enter, you stroll along a path covered with bark, and your first stop is a lily pond, smiling with the requisite lilies of various colors—if you're lucky, maybe even with a frog on top. For some unknown reason there's an odd-shaped rock embedded in the pavement surrounding the pond; I've always found it just the right place to pause for a moment's reflection. Then it's time to meander across the little wooden bridge—every garden should have one and hopefully a bubbling brook as well.

The paved path leads up toward the main area of the garden, and I have a choice: take the gravel path first or weave around to the rose garden. Since I like saving the best for last, I take the gravel path, enjoying a wide variety of wildflowers and herbs along the way, finally coming to a manmade pond where water plants coexist happily and Coy have been installed for color. A pond flows from a waterfall and the nearby gazebo makes a great place to sit and just listen to the water, letting the sounds of it wash your cares away, at least for a while. Then, turning back to the pavement, I stroll past the remnants of blue hydrangeas to my favorite place: the rose garden.

I should say "gardens," because this beautiful park has several of them. Trellises along this path weigh heavy with the blooms and scents of roses, and there's a lovely square fountain area where each corner hosts a trellis with its own variety of flowers and colors. Sitting in front of the fountain, a spitting lion, offers a perfect view of the downtown skyline of Fort Worth, a wonderful combination of natural and manmade beauty. The built-in benches provide a great place for reading or writing on a day when I have more time than I do right now.

The pull of the real world begins to draw me back down the path, under more trellises covered with roses and some with bright orange trumpet vine. I won't go too fast because I don't really want the walk to be over. Near the path leading to the bridge, I stop for a moment to remember each detail so I can take it with me back to my desk today. I leave with the fullness of nature's beauty in my heart and my head.

Today, I promise to stop and remember the fullness of a special place in nature when I feel the need for a place of beauty.

Exploring Busyness

Summer seems to be a time for being on the run. Despite the hot weather, long days and sunny skies compel us to work as much into one day as we can. Are you burning up the road with your busyness today? What aspects of your walk bring this to your attention? Are you walking faster than usual to get finished and on to other tasks? What might make you want to slow down? Has your creative work become "busyness" rather than impassioned prose? Read "Smokin'" as you consider your own busy life.

Smokin'

"Smokin'!"

—*The Mask*

The skies are overcast. But it's not fog and it's not clouds—believe it or not, it's smoke. Fires burning out of control in Central America and Mexico have blown these hazy days all the way to Texas! It's made a muggy, hazy end to what was otherwise a pretty lovely spring.

While I was taking my morning walk—and before I knew about the fires—I came up with another reason why our skies could have gone gray. I decided it was us down here below, polluting the air with our busyness and constant efforts to "do, do, do." "Smokin' up the roads of life with our hot-rod wheels."

Maybe because summer itself flows with such a power current of energy, I'm determined to do more than I possibly can in a twenty-four-hour period. Everything is fresh, blushing with possibility, and I've found myself caught up in it: working endless hours at a job I don't really enjoy while trying to convince myself I'm grateful for it, writing the stories I really want to write but can't get clear-headed enough to focus on, trying to live a life that's both balanced and serene in every area from food to fitness, while still making room to love and nourish those who need my love and nourishment on a daily basis. No wonder I'm tired—and if everyone else in the world is operating at this pace, no wonder the sky is smokin'.

As I walk today, I find myself wanting to stay focused on the things that are stable and calm in this world. The Bible tells us to study the lilies of the field, who have no care for tomorrow; there's a lot to be said for this attitude, even for those of us who have no religious affiliation. Don't the lilies truly have everything they need, and aren't they a beautiful vision for us to behold, without any effort at all on their part? Yet I can spend hours worrying about my appearance, shopping for things I don't need, trying to create a good facade, filling my head and my life with chaos and wasted energy. The seasons of the tree's life come and go as they will, while the tree stands by and watches as it all unfolds. How is it that the tree can know without knowing that it will always have only the spring, summer, fall, and winter, those and no more? What can be done and must be done will be done . . . that's all any tree can do. Why is it that I, with all my so-called knowledge, can't have the same understanding?

Of course, my world is a bit more complicated than that of a tree or a flower. But I could take a small lesson from the world that lives on the breath of Spirit. There are only so many hours in the day, and only so much that can be accomplished in a lifetime. The blooms, the scents, the leaves, the cool clear days will be gone all too soon. Take some deep breaths and relax. Walk with purpose, but also with consideration for the world that greets us with its stability every day. Truly, nothing is so important it won't keep till tomorrow.

Today, I will slow down and savor the scents, sounds, and sights of summer.

Exploring Conversations

Have you ever noticed how birds have their say, no matter what? As you walk today, listen to the conversations of birds in your area. What do they seem to be saying to each other? Can you understand and apply any of their conversations to your life? What strikes you about the mood of the conversations? Are you drawn more to the pleasant chatter or to the bickering brawls? Do other animals you might see on your daily jaunts have their own particular brands of dialogue? How can you use what you hear in your writing or life? Read "Bird Battles," then write about the conversations you hear during your own walk.

Bird Battles

The battle is to hold to the vision I know and must express, but the confidence to do it, where does that come from?
—Honor Moore

We could learn a thing or two by observing the way birds solve problems. Take, for instance, a mockingbird or a blue jay battling a cat. The cat is probably doing something that's detrimental to the bird's well-being (like trying to catch and eat it or its offspring, maybe!) and the bird takes the loudest and most aggressive stance possible to protect its boundaries. How many self-help books out there advise us humans to do the same thing?

Now I don't know about you, but I haven't had the best of luck with protecting my own boundaries. For years, I didn't even bother; I just went with the flow. Which reminds me of doves actually: they just sit on the ground, eat till they're stuffed, and don't ever get upset about much of anything, even the fat cat that pops in unexpectedly to disrupt their meal. Doves get eaten by cats quite often. That was me, the dove. Occasionally, I'd gather the gumption to quietly "coo" up some boundaries that either weren't taken seriously or were just plain ignored. Doves don't get very far with what they want and neither did I.

The birds I admire the most are the ones who bravely say what's on their mind. They don't seem to care what anybody's going to think. Some birds even go after friends and family members, too. I've seen an angry mockingbird perched prominently on a branch, squawking like a driver in bad traffic. Then without warning another mockingbird appears, starts buzzing the branch in midair warfare, finally unseating his fellow feathered friend. This bird-to-bird combat usually continues until one or the other leaves the scene in defeat. The battle doesn't seem to be territorial, but once it's over nobody's left on the scene. Who knows, maybe mockingbirds just enjoy a good tug-of-war every now and then?

Anyway, I decided that while I didn't necessarily want to start buzzing my opponent to my point across, I could at least get serious and say what I thought, point-blank, not rudely but plainly (unlike some of the more vocal bird species!). We'd probably all be a lot healthier if we just got those feelings out there instead of keeping them bottled up inside like toxic waste.

I've decided, though, that there's absolutely nothing wrong with the bird approach to life, and it's a perfectly good example for bringing out the best of the characters in my writing. I'm using my feathered friends' fine example of chitter and chatter to create strong assertive people as well as to become one of those people in my own life.

Today, I won't feel guilty about saying what I need to say to stay true to myself.

Exploring Ingenuity

Squirrels have their own ways of getting things done. Have you seen any squirrels on your walks lately? What were they doing? Did they seem busy or were they just chilling out and beating the summer heat? What kind of people do squirrels remind you of? Do you know any people like this? Maybe you're one of these people. How can you use ingenuity to accomplish things in your life? Read "Squirrel Ingenuity" and think about how you might apply such cleverness as part of your daily routine.

Squirrel Ingenuity

There is a correlation between the creative and the screwball. So we must suffer the screwball gladly.

—Kingman Brewster, Jr.

Maybe you haven't noticed, but squirrels have something of a screwball nature. They're almost always up to something and quite often it's something odd. Better yet, it's an unusual way of getting what they want.

Take the bird feeder, for instance. I've been keeping an eye on one particular feeder when I take my walk each day. The owner started out with a standard little plastic job, one of those feeders on a slender pole that you'd never imagine a squirrel finding any way to climb. Think again! There's always a way down, and the squirrels soon found free-falling from a nearby tree a great way to approach their meal. The owner thought he'd solved this dilemma by putting a rounded baffle on top of the feeder, but the clever critters decided it made a great slide. He moved the feeder and seems for a time to have found success, but my money's on the squirrels at this point. I fully expect them to be performing some kind of acrobatic feats to get to their birdseed goal by tomorrow. There's always the squirrel pyramid!

But squirrels know how to chill out, too. Have you ever seen one stretched out on a branch, flat as a carpet, sawing logs that Paul Bunyan couldn't cut in a week? Or what about those days when two of them are playing a chipper game of chase across the top of your yard, jumping from tree to roof to wire back to tree again.

When I think of my hectic days, I realize I don't have anything on the squirrels. Somehow, they manage to get it all done and still have time for naps and fun. My stress level suggests that I might be wise to take a lesson here. Somehow, I've managed to squeeze lots of work in but I seem to have forgotten the fun, and the last time I had a nap was probably when I was about twelve.

I need to take a lesson from the squirrel family about finding an easier way to get things done—or, if not easier, at least more fun! For instance, I could always take that reading to the coffeehouse or out to the back porch, instead of holing myself up in the office. I might even consider just opening the windows for a change, and letting some of the fresh outside air come inside. I could move to the front room, where it's sunnier and brighter and, well, just different. Maybe I just need to completely stop working for the afternoon and indulge myself in a nap or a walk in the park. The squirrels would find a way to make it work, and there's no reason I can't do the same.

Today, I'm going to bring fun into my work, and I'm also going to remember to take a nap!

Exploring Responsibility

Do you notice more stray animals in your neighborhood at one time of year than another? How many strays have you seen around this summer? How does it make you feel to see abandoned animals? Is there anything you can do—or want to do—to help them? How do animals live when no one cares for them? Read my experiences in "Cats Abound" and think about what your own response to a situation like this might be. How does responsibility play a part in your creative life? How is it possible to be a responsible creator?

Cats Abound

No art can develop until it permeates deeply into the life of the people.
—Meridel Le Sueur

It's been raining cats around my neighborhood lately! Although I'm definitely a cat person, I have to admit the abundance of my furry friends on the streets has been driving me a little nuts.

Last month I rescued five black kitties someone had abandoned in a field I pass on my walk every day. At first I didn't realize there were five of them—I thought there were two. The next day I saw two more, and the following day, another one. By the time I realized there were five of them, I'd already committed myself to catching them and trying to get them adopted. I realized it wasn't going to be an easy task.

Every day, I'd take food and water to the spot where they'd been left, and they'd run out like little demons, eager for their morning meal. Catching the first three was easy—these kittens seemed to have been around humans, and once I got them back to my garage they turned out to be little softies. The last two were more problematic, needing to be coaxed again and again, with more exotic kinds of fancy cat food; and the fifth one was a real bugger. That one took days and finally a trap to catch! But eventually I had them all rounded up and tucked away in the garage.

Except for the reflecting that haunts me even now: how many more kittens are left to die because people don't want to be responsible for them? Not even for taking them to a humane society, where at least their long-term suffering could be averted. Whatever happened to the idea that people had to be responsible for what they created in their lives? Seems like most people just live for what suits them these days, and if it doesn't suit them, it's time to get rid of it, be it material things, people, or pets.

Many of us believe, like Thoreau, that we're in this world "not chiefly to make this a good place to live in, but to live in it, be it good or bad." Perhaps for some of us, a life well-lived provides satisfaction enough. But for others—myself included—living well means being aware of what's happening around us and doing our part, however small, to make this world a better place to live in. In A *Return to Love*, Marianne Williamson writes that "we're all assigned a piece of the garden, a corner of the universe that is ours to transform." As individuals, we are presented every day with unique opportunities to take an active role in the transformation of our world—as I had an opportunity to do in making sure five little kittens found happy homes instead of starving to death abandoned on a roadside. As artists, we have a different kind of opportunity to participate in this transformation—by putting work into the world that makes others aware then perhaps more willing to become active themselves in the process of creating positive change. The part we play, as individuals or as artists, is never too small if it changes the path of one soul for the better.

Oh, I forgot to mention—doing my part didn't end there. Two weeks after the little critters had moved on, I looked out my back door and saw a mother cat with three baby kittens in my backyard! These girls are still looking for homes—but they've had their shots, their tubes tied, and at least they're still getting a decent meal every day. My friend tells me it's no good trying to avoid stray cats—once they know you're gullible, they find you!

Today I intend to take my responsibilities seriously in my writing and my life.

Exploring Balance

There's something special about hummingbirds, isn't there? Do you have them in your area? Have you tried putting out a feeder to attract these delicate but aggressive little creatures? Do you know where to look for them while you're walking? Have you trained your eyes to be sharp enough to spot them? Do you ever find yourself aggressive in the workplace, protective of yourself and your territory? How can this be both a good and a bad thing? How do you balance aggressiveness with acceptance? Why is it sometimes necessary to be aggressive in protecting our creative space? Read "Hummingbird House" and see if you agree.

Hummingbird House

It is not enough to be busy . . . The question is: what are we busy about?
—Henry David Thoreau

Hummingbirds fascinate me, but it's an odd sort of attraction. I love to watch them—delicate bodies held aloft by invisible wings; long slender beaks seeking out sugar feeders for the energy that keeps them going; perched on minuscule twigs like tiny despots protecting their territory; bathing themselves on a wire during a summer shower. These tiny little creatures boast more energy and aggressiveness than birds five times their size. In the area where I live they only visit for a couple of months during the summer, but the feeder is always up and ready for them long before they finally arrive. I could sit and watch them for hours, strategiz-ing how they'll keep "their" territory safe. You'd think they'd work together since they're so small and vulnerable, but I never saw a bird more determined to take care of itself.

Visiting California last summer provided me with a special treat—the hummingbirds live there year-round and when I took my daily walk, they became a part of it. In fact, I couldn't take a walk out there without seeing and hearing the hummingbirds. It takes a sharp eye to actually see them when you're walking, because they don't rest in one spot for long. But they're louder than you'd think, so I just followed the rapping sound of their sharp little bird calls until my gaze found them. Watching them flit from one beautiful flowering tree to the next, so many different varieties that I had no clue what I was looking at—purple flowers, red powderpuffs, slender orange tubes—added an exotic flavor to my daily walk.

But regardless of how much I enjoy these splendid little creatures, I've finally come to the conclusion that they aren't very nice birds. They're determined, territorial, and sometimes just plain mean. They dive and buzz any and every bird who even thinks about entering their territory, and even though I've heard it's really soft, that pointed little beak looks pretty dangerous when it's aimed straight at you. Hummers aren't about to share any part of what they've got with anybody else. Maybe you've got to be that way when you're the smallest bird in the sky. Maybe it's just survival.

Watching hummingbirds makes me think about the idea of balance. Certainly there are times to put all that energy and aggressiveness into action, but if you've ever watched a hummer guarding a feeder, you understand that these little beggars don't seem to know when to give it a rest. How many other birds have you seen protecting the food source this way? Normally, everybody takes turns eating their fair share. In real-ity, there's plenty for everyone. Hummers don't seem to realize it's okay to chill out sometimes and let a few other birds take a turn at the sugar water. They may be small birds, but their big ego doesn't have much compassion for other hungry beaks.

Still, hummers provide me with a prime opportunity to observe just how powerful and charismatic the small can be. Everybody loves hummingbirds, in spite of their bossy little ways. Being strong about what you want doesn't necessarily mean that people won't like you, and that's a pretty good thing to know for those of us who have trouble protecting our boundaries. Protecting and seeking out one's space is important, especially one's creative space, which sometimes other people don't recognize as sacred and delicate. Likewise, the delicate beauty of the hummers is worth the time it takes to seek them out. Then, it's fun to remember as you watch them that's there's nothing really delicate about these tiny wonders at all!

Sometimes life offers contrasts we aren't expecting. Today, I'll seek out balance in that contrast.

Exploring Tolerance

"To each his own" is a familiar phrase, but how tolerant are you of others and their mannerisms and idiosyncrasies? What examples do you see as you walk of tolerance in the natural world? What part does tolerance play in your own life, and how do you deal with differences between yourself and others? Does anything in particular capture your feelings about tolerance on your walk today? How do you approach this topic in your creative work? Think about the idea as you read "Go with the Flow."

Go with the Flow

Try to find your deepest issue in every confusion, and abide by that.
—D. H. Lawrence

A recent trip away from home found me falling in love with a new city: San Antonio, Texas. New walks with new sights and faces are always a treat, but this magical city makes every day seem like a fiesta. Early mornings found me strolling the river walkways near the place I was staying, where elegant homes backed up to the cement-walled river winding its way through the area. Farsighted townswomen, seeking to protect their city from future flooding, promoted the containment of this river's waters in the early 1900s. The old homes backing up to the river have seen its boundaries change from sloping dirt banks to landscaped terraces.

Walking those paths early on a summer morning intoxicates like nowhere else I know of in the state of Texas. Birdsong fills the air—the gentle cooing of doves punctuated by the trills and melodies of a myriad of other songbirds. Scents fight for control of my senses—flowering trees and shrubs, flowers too numerous to name, kitchen scents wafting from open windows and doors. Sights abound—the deep velvety emerald green of the water and the flowers spilling like a pitcher of fruity sangria from the backyards of the houses. All growing, glowing, existing together in a harmony of natural wonder.

Morning walks turn to midday and evening walks, and the river moves from neighborhoods to downtown. During the city's development for the HemisFair in the late sixties, the water-lined walkways were further landscaped and developed, so now the entire downtown area is a stroll along the river. Following my day's activities, I continue on with the flow of the water. The river courses beside downtown streets, bordered for a time by sidewalk eateries and shops, throngs of people strolling or enjoying boat rides, and hotels with balconies overlooking the cheery scenes below.

Walking these paths refreshed me with energy and enthusiasm found only in cities like this, where the downtown area teems with people and life. Perhaps because of the river, the water of life flowing through this town and cleansing it daily, an aura of tolerance prevails. Not only do plants of innumerable different varieties grow in harmony along the riverbanks, apparently people grow in harmony, too. San Antonio is as culturally diverse as any city I've ever known, yet there's a lot of smiling and the faces beam as brightly as those cheery gardens I noticed early in the day. Everybody seems to be going with the flow.

Today, I'll practice going with the flow, no matter where I happen to be.

Exploring New Horizons

Pay attention to people working in their gardens. What kinds of tasks are they doing? If you don't see any people, what kinds of gardens do you see? Are flowers planted in beds or borders, or do some of your neighbors have their plants in pots? What thoughts and creative ideas does garden work bring to your mind? Does some repotting need to be done in your own life? Read "Repotting" for one way of looking at the subject.

Repotting

Our aspirations are our possibilities.

—Samuel Johnson

Summer finds gardens in full bloom. (Unless they're struggling to stay alive, as they do in Texas!) People have all sorts of gardens; one of my neighbors has a lot of her plants in large ceramic pots. I love walking by her house, where the painted colors offer some stiff competition to what's actually growing in the pots. It's a feast for the eyes!

When I walked by one day recently, she was doing some serious repotting, moving plants that had outgrown their containers to bigger pots, replacing dirt to give the rest of them a new lease on life. Pots and potting soils of various types littered her lawn and driveway. Dirt covered her arms like long gloves and she even had a smudge on her nose. It looked like a pretty thankless job to me, and I said as much.

"No way," she laughed. "There's nothing like getting in the dirt to make you feel like a kid again. The plants get what they need and so do I."

Maybe for her, repotting simply presented a means of playing in the dirt. Or perhaps gardening was something more—a means of changing everything without ever leaving home. The plants get room to let their roots spread and grow and so does my neighbor. But sometimes, I decided, people need repotting on a bigger scale.

Last summer, for instance, I spent three months in Los Angeles. I felt like a new person, even though I knew the move was only temporary. Somehow, though, I knew I'd outgrown the state where I was born and raised, the people in my life, maybe even my life itself.

I'm still longing, I'm afraid, but I'm beginning to seriously work on changing my situation. It's amazing how great that kind of expansion can feel: you stand taller, feel lighter, and you bloom. Until I can get on with the repotting itself, I try to find other ways to experience change—doing something a different way, taking a little weekend trip, reading books about places I've never been. Even repotting a few houseplants! It's not quite as good as making the big leap to a new place, but almost—at least it provides a chance for me to slow down and think about steps I can take to start repotting in my own life. So don't underestimate the power of new soil: even a little goes a long way.

Today, I'll take another step toward my dream of repotting my life.

Exploring Stillness

How do you deal with the hot days of summer? Do you find a way to continue walking, even when it's hot enough to melt the rubber on the soles of your shoes? How does the heat change the way you see the world? How are your walks different when it's hot? What might you see that you wouldn't see otherwise? How does life in general change when the temperature is at the top of the thermometer? Do you find it seems a little cooler when you stay still? How does that stillness affect both you and your work? Read "The Heat Is On" and think about ways you can slow down this summer.

The Heat Is On

In times like these, it helps to recall that there have always been times like these.

—Paul Harvey

Here in Texas, it's sizzling. We don't just have hot days, we've got scorchers. This summer, the scorchers have been worse than usual, without even a summer shower to break the monotony. Everything's dying and some of us are about to tear our hair out. "When will it end?" has become the mantra of my walk. If I never saw brown again, I could live happy for the rest of my life!

What's all this about, I ask myself day after day as I pour water on my yard and down my parched throat after my daily trek. I'm sure nature has a plan, but I'm not exactly sure what it is.

Today, something came to me I hadn't considered before. What does heat, what does drought force life to do? It forces everything to STOP. No more life, no more dashing about (well, unless you want heat rash and possibly a heart attack). Things stop and you'd better follow along if you know what's good for you.

Nature has a plan for heat and drought as well as everything else. Granted, we may be mucking up that plan to some extent with all the pollution we're contributing to the environment, but let's assume for now that nature still has the upper hand. Plants pull back deep down into their root system when things get too difficult on the surface; birds and animals know when it's time to curl up in the shade and nap. Maybe we can't afford to take things as casually as they do, but we can certainly slow down.

Instead, when things are hot and heavy with summer humidity, we dash about as if we don't know any better, trying to accomplish more and more, regardless of how high the thermometer or our blood pressure climbs. We don't even consider the possibility that maybe these hot days are saying, "Hey, why don't you slow down a little? Stay still and cool off." Instead, we just turn the air conditioner a notch higher and pick up the pace even more.

Why not get up a little earlier tomorrow and enjoy the day while there's still a little freshness to it? After your walk, you might have time for reading the paper and drinking a second cup of coffee, a chance to meditate or read a daily devotional. You might find a new idea in the stillness, or the answer to a particularly trying problem in your writing. Taking that early walk on a summer morning doesn't speed up my day; it slows it down and puts everything in perspective. Suddenly, I realize the heat is really a blessing in disguise, and the drought—well, all things come to an end in their own time. Rain will come.

I pace myself in the heat of a summer day, and am grateful for the chance to slow my life down.

Exploring Fear

What kinds of bugs and insects do you see when you're walking? When you encounter something unusual, does it frighten or excite you? Why? How do you face your fears? Have you ever wondered if bugs and insects have fears? How might they face them? Could you apply any of those ideas in your own life, or in your writing? In what ways? Now read "Arachnophobia," and then as you walk today, consider how you confront your own fears.

Arachnophobia

The only thing we have to fear is fear itself.
—Franklin Delano Roosevelt

I have a mild fear of spiders. Nothing that sends me running for the covers of my bed, just a creepy sensation: I wouldn't want those hairy legs crawling on me. So while my recent encounter with a tarantula wasn't totally terrifying, it was slightly earthshaking.

I've seen them before in my area—our home is near a nature preserve and "wild" creatures have been known to creep out of it from time to time. I wasn't surprised to see the spider, but I was surprised that I actually took the time to stop and stare at it for a while. I have this unreasonable certainty that spiders and snakes can jump and run, so if you get too close you're liable to find yourself fighting them off. It's unreasonable, as I said, but since I'm writing about nature and how what we find has implications in our lives, I decided I couldn't pass by this opportunity to consider the tarantula.

So I watched it walk. Well, the walking didn't happen right away. When I first approached the massive black arachnid, it curled itself up into a tight fist and just sat there, daring me to come closer but not really doing anything to defend itself. I guess it finally got bored or maybe just reassured by my distance: it unfurled itself and proceeded to cross the street. Its big hairy body moved along slowly, inching its way across the pavement like a wayward caterpillar, testing each movement with one of those skinny black legs. I found its movement both fascinating and terrifying.

When I tired of watching, I turned to go, leaving my newfound friend with its journey about half complete, wondering how long it would take to reach the safety of the woods. My question was soon answered: when I looked back to check its pace, the tarantula was gone. How could it have disappeared so fast? For a moment I wondered if I'd actually imagined the entire encounter!

What message did that gigantic spider have for me? I silently wondered as I resumed my walk home. What could I take back with me from today's meeting? Was there something in my writing I was afraid to confront? That spider had been afraid too. Both of us had confronted our fears, however. We'd moved beyond them in order to move on.

Today I'll take a moment to confront a fear, knowing I'll grow stronger and more confident for having done it.

Exploring Deeper Issues

When you walk, do you focus on what's ahead of you, or do you watch where you're walking? Keeping focused on each step along the way has its advantages, especially if you live in an older area with lots of cracks in the sidewalk. Are you careful to avoid the cracks, or do they often trip you up? What seems to cause these cracks? Do cracks in the sidewalk remind you of any issues in your own life? What are they, and how might you choose to deal with them? Do you ever allow yourself to explore those cracks creatively? In what ways? Read "Watch Your Step!" and then write about what trips you up.

Watch Your Step!

Only the heart knows how to find what is precious.
—Fyodor Dostoyevsky

Walking in my neighborhood can be potentially hazardous to one's health. Although the massive old trees are a blessing during the summer heat, the sidewalks suffer their growth by splitting apart. The resulting rises and falls in the pavement can be dangerous if you don't watch where you're walking. More than once I've taken a gigantic trip—luckily I always manage to catch myself before hitting the cement.

It's interesting to consider the damage roots can do to something as seemingly impenetrable as concrete. Right before my eyes is the proof: the hardened product lifted right out of the ground as if it's been hit by an earthquake rather than by years of steady pressure. Years of constant push, push, push until finally the sidewalk itself bursts out of the ground like rubber. Which is why I've learned to pay attention to where I'm walking—while walking and while living.

One instant you'll be whistling along your merry way and the next you're flat-out shocked that you didn't realize your life was falling apart while you were planning next year's menu. Cracks in the sidewalk can turn up suddenly or they can be the result of years of root pushing. In life, maybe the crack is something as simple as forgetting a friend's birthday because you're particularly busy at work right now; but it can also be as big as your spouse having an affair that's been going on for months and you're missing all the signs of it.

Walking these wonderful old neighborhoods, I've learned to look at what's coming up on the horizon, to move toward it with excitement and anticipation. But I've also learned to pay attention to where each foot falls, to be in the moment on a walk or in my life. One never knows where a dangerous crack in the cement may turn up. When I'm watching where I step, nine times out of ten I can stop the fall before I go down.

Sometimes the cracks in our lives provide great opportunities for stories, or for exploring emotions we'd rather not look at. The cracks along the way today have made me realize I want to touch the deeper issues in my writing, and to do that I need to pay attention to the deeper issues in my life.

Today, I'll take each moment as it comes, looking deeper into the issues at hand, considering what implications the moment may hold not only for the future, but for the present as well.

Exploring Smells

What comes to your mind when walking after a rain? Do you notice the difference in the way the air smells? What's different about your walk after a rain? Can you describe it, making use of all your senses, or does one stand out more than another? How do you feel after a rain? What feelings do you bring home from the walk with you? Do you have trouble incorporating smell into your writing? How can being more aware of smells help you? Read "After the Rain," then write about what tickles your nostrils today.

After the Rain

We may not need smell to survive, but without it we feel lost and disconnected.

—Diane Ackerman

Maybe the sun is supposed to shine after the rain, but all I really noticed on my walk today was the smell. There's an almost indescribable quality about that smell, and it seems to change from rain to rain. What I decided, though, was that everything comes together after a rainstorm—air, water, earth, sky. It's like stirring the pot of some splendid concoction and the smell that fills the air—well, some days it's a preview of heaven and others you're not sure if God's gotten the recipe quite right.

Today, for instance, after a long, looonnnggg spell without rain, the smell was distinctive, to say the least. With so many plants already dead, the smell took on a kind of musky, smoky, dead aroma that wasn't completely displeasing but twisted your nostrils all the same. If you captured that smell and bottled it, you'd definitely need some pretty ingenious ploys to market it. But some people love it, my husband for one. He tells me it reminds him of something that's burned and gotten wet, which for some reason appeals to him.

Personally, I'd rather have one of those days when the rain has washed everything clean, when what you smell after a downpour is green, light, and fresh. On those days, flowers smell sweeter than expensive perfume; grass smells newly bottled and ready for sale; even the dirt smells freshly unearthed. I like the idea that the old has somehow been washed away, and the world's all spiffed up for a celebration. The musky burning wet stuff just makes me think it wasn't clean to begin with and the storm hasn't made things much better.

But those are the rains we need the most, so I take the slightly disagreeable smell along with the blessing of the showers. Walking along paths that are still slightly damp and puddle-strewn, noticing how plants along the way stand a little taller than they did the day before, makes the dead smell not only tolerable but actually somewhat pleasant. I consider that I've been avoiding writing about smell, and probably missing a good chance to add this element of sensory material to my stories. Suddenly, I'm remembering smells I noticed earlier—the tiny flowers on the holly bush at the corner of my house emitting a sweet smell I'd never noticed before, the smell of frying onions from my neighbor's kitchen, the dog poop I nearly stepped in just outside my gate.

What things might I compare to such a smell as the one I encountered today, which is so different from anything else I can think of? A dead rotting smell like hay in a damp barn. Maybe to say that "nothing smells like a dry day in Texas after a rainstorm" is the most accurate description of all.

Today, I'll notice unusual smells around me, and think about the ways they might compare to something else.

Exploring Abundance

What examples of summer's abundance do you see in the area where you live and walk? How many such examples can you find on your walk today? How does summer's abundance influence your life on a daily basis? How does it influence your creative life? What's your favorite aspect of summer's abundance? Read "Overflowing Grace," then consider as you walk how such abundance directly influences your life.

Overflowing Grace

You live only once—but if you work it right, once is enough.
—Joe E. Lewis

As summer draws to a close, my reflections as I walk turn to its abundance. I can't help but think with a little sad irony that sometimes summer goes a little overboard in its generosity. This year, for example, my area has seen too many abandoned kittens, more than a hundred days with no rain in sight, and gardens withering away from the drought. During my walks, I've felt a lot of frustration about the place where I live.

Today, however, I pushed the negativity aside and turned my focus to some of the more pleasant graces of these past summer months, of the blessings I've found in unexpected yet ordinary places—"everyday epiphanies" as Pat Conroy refers to them in *The Prince of Tides*. Blessings like a waft of scent on the breeze from the sweet olive tree growing near the kitchen door; like the rainbow prism of light reflected through my neighbor's sprinkler as I pass her house; like the red glow of a cardinal through the trees on a dreary day.

On my walk today, I see that the green stuff in my neighborhood is starting to look a little happier with fall on the horizon. I haven't seen one stray cat today, and the ground is still a little damp from last week's rain. As for me, I feel good about my accomplishments, about the things I've done and learned this summer, about the fact that I've continued my walks even on days when all I wanted to do was sit by the air conditioner.

Mostly, I'm thankful that I still have a place to walk, and even though it may not have the best temperature in the world or be the most beautiful location in the country, there's always something to smile about. Like the squirrel that fell flat out of the tree during a skirmish with its cousin, or the mockingbird fighting a battle of its own with a grasshopper, or the friendly dog that decided to join me for a few blocks.

Grace overflows in summer in a whole world of ways—in the fullness of the trees, the colors of the garden, and the merriment of the birds. Grace spills into my life with lessons about life that only come around during this particular season. I'm thankful for the blessings of summer, even if they aren't always exactly what I was expecting or hoping for!

Today, I greet the last days of summer with a smile and say a prayer of gratitude for its bounty.

The Wonders of Walking

Fall Explorations

Now that you're inspired and focused and feeling full of summer's abundance, fall is the time to begin putting your goals and plans into action. Every productive and creative venture requires discipline, which is often the hardest aspect of the task. But fall is the perfect time to get to work. The weather is cool and crisp; the days are calling for action and movement.

As you enter fall, what do you want to accomplish? Is the path to your goal clearly laid out? What is it about fall that makes you want to get moving, to accomplish things you've been putting off all summer? How does this season make you feel when you step outside? Does the beauty of the rich autumn colors and rapidly approaching quiet and calm of winter inspire you to move ahead with creative projects? Fall beckons with cool arms and moments for reflection, but also provides many opportunities for discipline and advancement. Fall is a time for getting ready.

As you step into the motion of this season and begin your journey in earnest, you'll be doing so with purpose and passion. The risks you take in fall will unleash in you a sense of courage as you move along your path. Fill your days with fall's fullness, but don't forget this is a wonderful time for pruning as well as planning. Look deep inside and reflect on your emotions, the positive and the negative. For every creative soul, there's much to be found in fall's abundance.

Exploring Purpose

What are the colors of fall in the area where you live? When was the last time you watched fall leaves, noticing the way they dance and play like children? How does fall make you feel about the cycles of life? Does walking on a crisp autumn day, watching leaves fall, lead to thoughts about your own life's purpose? What steps are you taking right now to accomplish this purpose? What do you want to accomplish creatively? Read "Fall Leaves Fall" and then reflect on the uniqueness of your own life.

Fall Leaves Fall

Always be a first-rate version of yourself, instead of a second-rate version of somebody else.
—Judy Garland

Fall happens to be one of my favorite times of year, which is unfortunate since Texas isn't known for its lengthy autumns. What we get here is sort of a mini-version of the season—just enough to let you know what you're missing! Still, I manage to make do with what I've got.

The leaves may be slow to turn in this part of the country but their final dance to earth is just the same as anywhere else. The little ones, oaks and ash, scurry and twirl together with vibrant urgency; midsized pecan and cottonwood stray along as if they had all the time in the world; and the largest, sycamore and sweet gum, take this final waltz alone, delicately using every last bit of grace as they trail their way down, down, down to reunite once more with Mother Earth. Some make their way in silence, drifting on breezes in full contemplation; others are caught by a wind and chatter gaily—swisck, swisck, swisck—as they dance and fall. Each one—every single leaf—has its own individuality.

As I walk, watching the leaves slowly turn luscious autumn shades and then begin the imminent fall, I am reminded again of the miraculous cycle of life. We are each given a limited amount of time—some much less than others—to plant our garden and shape our world. As infants, we wait tentatively in the love and protection of our parents' arms, yearning for the day when we've grown to fullness and are invited to participate in life's day. In youth, we bend and sway with the winds of life, proudly displaying knowledge we haven't yet earned or learned. Like the fall leaves, it is only when we come to maturity, toward the middle and end of our lives, that we are truly able to contemplate the dance we will leave to the memory of others.

The dance brings with it finality, a rejoining of our individual self with the oneness of nature. It is not something to be feared, but rather embraced as a glorious slash of color across the canvas of a life well lived. Whether we make our dance joyful and energetic or silent and delicately graceful isn't important. What matters is that we enter into it fully, with complete devotion to some purpose beyond ourselves. Our imprint upon the world can be as individual as each leaf—like no other.

Today, as you walk, consider the imprint you would like to leave behind. Will your dance be remembered as a joyous one, filled with cheerfulness and urgency, or will you be a silent partner in the round, one who gives and works behind the scenes? Will your branches stretch far, casting cover that touches the lives of many, or will the precious garden you shade be your community and your family?

The final dance lies in wait for each of us. It is up to us to decide the purpose of our journey.

Today, I will watch the leaves as they waltz their way to earth, and consider the dance I would like my life to be.

Exploring Planning

Animals recognize the need to plan for winter. What plans are you making to ready yourself for your own future? Do you get a sense of urgency in the fall, an awareness that it's time to be preparing for what's to come? As you walk, what do you notice that indicates change? How do you feel about change? What part does planning play in your creative life? Read "Getting Ready" and then think about the preparations you want to make for the days ahead.

Getting Ready

In tomorrow walks today.

—Samuel Taylor Coleridge

I've been taking evening walks lately, and I've seen some strange things. Everybody in the animal kingdom seems to be getting ready for winter naps. When I walk along the road by the nature preserve near my home, I sometimes see raccoons, opossums, and once even a skunk rummaging in leftover garbage from the homes nearby, fat and happy and ready to sleep off that extra weight. If only I could be so lucky!

Sometimes these animals do a little more than just load up their bodies for winter—they seek out just the wrong places for their naps. Not long ago, a skunk tried to take up residence under our own house, and it took a lot of coaxing and a can of cat food to get him out of there without a big stink! I guess the little fellow decided he'd rather spend his winter as somebody's houseguest rather than all alone in some rotten tree trunk.

Raccoons and skunks aren't the only ones storing up for sleep either—the squirrels have been having a field day lately, planting nuts in every corner of the garden in case they wake up and need a little snack or food is sparse come spring.

Of course, the truth of the matter is that animals don't really hibernate here in Texas—it never gets cold enough for that. They do, however, sleep more than usual, and they do seem to plan on sleeping a lot. Animals have the best attitude in that they know how to live in the moment yet still keep busy with planning for the days ahead. Their planning involves more than just thinking about what they're going to do, though; it involves actually getting off their butts and doing what needs to be done.

Their flurry of preparatory activity makes me realize that as a writer I've got to remember to plan for what's ahead in order to achieve the desired outcome. What do I want to accomplish over the next few days, or months, or even years? It takes a long time to write a book, or a screenplay, or even a story, so by setting realistic steps toward my long-term goals, I'll be able to accomplish what I want to accomplish. The plan is simply part of the journey, and while I want to enjoy the journey, knowing I've made provisions for the outcome will make it all the more rewarding.

Today, I'll think about where I'm headed and what I'll need for my journey toward success.

Exploring Colors

Fall brings lots of gray days, but if you look close enough, you'll notice they aren't really all that gray. On your walk today, take time to notice how the gray skies bring out different shades of color in the world around you. Filmmakers often find gray days the best for shooting, since the muted light actually brings out richer colors than a sunny sky. What are some of your favorite fall colors, and what differences do you notice in them on a gray day? What shades of color do you use in your creative work? What kind of mood are you able to create with color? Read "The Colors of Gray" and then decide how you can enrich the colors of your own life when you're not feeling as sunny and bright as usual.

The Colors of Gray

I do have to force myself but once I get into it it's a pleasure. Why is it that it's so difficult when I know what a pleasure it will be?
—Alix Kates Shulman

Resistance pulled at me like a child begging to stay home from school. Cloudy gray skies overshadowed my usual enthusiasm for my morning walk. Where were the sunny days of summer—or at least the crisp bright mornings of an Indian summer? Today, it seemed, I was out of luck.

I started out on my normal trek feeling disheartened and thankless. My writing wasn't going well and the gray day wasn't helping one bit.

Then I began to notice things. I noticed the deep red of a rose that was wilting under the strain of a slight morning frost, and reddish-purple petals strewn across the sidewalk from the last brilliant stand of a neighboring shrub. I noticed twenty shades of muted green in the grass and leaves, various shades of white magnificence on the houses, bright surprises in the oranges of pumpkins set outside on people's steps, and a crayon box of cars parked along the street.

Little by little, I noticed the life flowing back into me. My spirits brightened, and joy filled up my heart and spilled over so that I found myself smiling, at the colors, at the day, at myself (and at anybody who happened to pass me along the way!). I started to ask myself why I'd been so dismal in the first place. Just because it was gray outside didn't mean it had to be gray inside me. Then I started to think about how I often take on somebody else's colors instead of paying attention to my own.

With heart and eyes open, I turned and started on my way back home. As I went, I tried to take in as many of the "colors" of gray as possible. The deep blue sheen of the jay like a touch of acrylic on its feathers, the earthy richness of a terra-cotta birdbath in my neighbor's backyard, a sunny patch of fabric hanging in her window like the promise of brighter days to come. I took these images in deep, and as a result, when I opened the door of my house I was hit with such a vibrancy of hues I knew my own gray mood had melted away into a rainbow of life. I took up my work, refreshed and ready to begin anew.

Today, I'll meet gray skies with a smile, for I know they hide colors that will brighten me inside and out, flowing over into my writing and filling it with new life.

Exploring Courage

What messages of hope and courage does nature offer to you? Do you take time to listen? Are you able to carry those messages back into your routine? What do you see when you look into water, or a mirror? Do you face yourself with courage, or do you feel frustration about the path you are walking? How do you show courage in your creative work? Read "Around the Lake" and think about a message of courage that might be offered to you as you walk today.

Around the Lake

Everyone has talent. What is rare is the courage to follow that talent to the dark place where it leads.

—Erica Jong

There's nothing more wonderful than a walk in a new place. The place I've retreated to this weekend has a lake, and it's wonderful to be able to circle its shores and stare mesmerized into the mirrorlike water. When something shatters its stillness, though, I'm reminded of my reason for being here: need to get away from my routine, from issues and problems and daily frustrations.

Sometimes I get so discouraged when walking my artist's path, tired of all the frustrations and fewness of the successes. Sometimes it seems as if I try and try, but never reach the place where I really want to be with

my work. Sometimes I feel like I'm shattered—split into a million frag-
ments that include trying to find time to be creative in the middle of a
life that requires regular work to pay the bills and spending too much
time with others. All those things that living in the real world seems to
require.

I stare into the lake, peaceful, smooth, and I try to find some of that
peace inside myself. I remind myself the way of the artist isn't an easy
one, and it's okay to turn back at any time and slip onto the road most
people choose to walk, where questions about why you're doing what
you're doing are the exception rather than the norm. I could go back and
walk that road, couldn't I? Or is that the road that would shatter me as I
try to hold back all the things I want to say, need to say, that my soul
aches to share with a world that isn't really interested in listening?

As I come around another bend in the path, I stop to inhale a breath
of the morning and ask the lake what message it has for me. The flip of
a fish catches my eye, rippling the lake. Then, as easily as that, I know
what message the lake wants to share. It's a message of hope and promise and courage, and it's waiting for me where before I saw only despair
and frustration. What I can see now is that the lake isn't like a mirror at
all. The lake is water, fluid and smooth and unbreakable—and so am I.
Water always returns to calm and peace and certainty—and so can I.

*I am unbreakable, and I'll remember the lake when I feel uncertain about
my path.*

Exploring Risk-Taking

What kind of risks do you take in life? Are your walks always the same, or do you vary your route? Are you comfortable with taking risks? What are some risks you'd like to take? Do you take creative risks? In what ways? Read "Across the Green," then write about your own feelings about risk-taking.

Across the Green

True risk, that sudden leap into cold water, can carry you into a state of grace.

—Sting

Fall is a good time to walk on golf courses. I love to walk across the greens; they're always carefully landscaped, and the trail is paved and well kept. I can't always say the same for the sidewalks. Still, walking a course is risky—you've got to be careful or you're liable to wind up with a golf ball imprint on your forehead.

Sometimes, though, it's important to take risks. You can put them off till the time is right, but usually a risk is still a risk. But no matter how many times I've walked across golf courses, I've never actually been hit by a golf ball.

I always seem to try and put off taking risks in my life for as long as possible. Something may be eating at me for days, or months, or maybe even years, but will I deal with it the minute the nagging appears—heavens no! I'll wait until whatever point I've determined is virtually risk-free and only then will I do what I need to do. Many times, what I've discovered is that what I've been putting off is something wonderful and I sure wished I'd done it a lot sooner.

Like waiting to go live in L.A., for instance. I put that one off for at least ten years, worried about this, worried about that, and when I finally got there I discovered life in L.A. is just like life anywhere else except for a couple of simple little things like perfect weather and the beach! You'd think I might have learned something by now, yet I continue to avoid taking risks, even though I could be enjoying the beauty of a lovely green or the blue of the Pacific Ocean. Even driving in traffic, which I'd been truly terrified to do, proved no different from driving the freeways near my home in Texas.

The bad part is, life is short, and it promises to end before I've taken all the risks I'd like to take. Many people discover how short life is the hard way—I don't want to be one of those people. In *A Man's Journey to Simple Abundance* by Sarah Ban Breathnach, essayist Sting says that "maybe risk is destiny . . . it makes sense because risk is the only thing that forces spiritual and emotional growth so immediately, so dramatically." If my destiny lies along the path of risk, I'm determined to walk that path.

So maybe walking the green isn't providing much of a risk right now—though there's always that group of fall golfers to watch out for. But I'm determined to look for bigger risks, to take that dive into the cold water, in both my writing and life in general. And since I've already spent so much time putting things off, there's no day like today to begin.

Today I'll look for ways to take a risk that might bring positive changes into my life.

Exploring Frustration

Some of us live in places where the seasons aren't very well defined. If you live in such a place, do you miss the seasons? How do you deal with this frustration? Do you seek out activities or images that bring the season to mind? How do you deal with such frustrations in your creative life? If the "season" of writing is avoiding you, how do you deal with your frustration? Read "Whatever Happened to Indian Summer?" then see what inspirations you find on your walk today to help you deal with creative frustration.

Whatever Happened to Indian Summer?

Life's under no obligation to give us what we expect.
—Margaret Mitchell

I could probably count the times I've experienced Indian summer. It just doesn't happen that much in the state of Texas. Which is a real disappointment since it's probably my favorite time of year. Earlier this week, as I was taking my daily walk on a muggy gray November day, I couldn't help but feel really frustrated that I don't live in a place with real seasons, or at least one where the season of fall happens more than once every ten years. The fact that I don't need to spend a lot of money on a winter wardrobe doesn't help ease my frustration at all.

Unfortunately, there's really nothing I can do to change the weather.

I can certainly visit other places and have the experience of fall, or I can surround myself with images that remind me of fall, or at the extreme, I could move. But for the moment, I simply have to accept the fact that this is the way it is and wait for it to pass.

I guess it's the same with any frustration. I can plan changes or make drastic changes, but these things often take time, and sometimes you just have to ride the frustration out. With writing, or any creative effort, it's often frustrating as you wait for your work to find its way to people who will appreciate your efforts. You long for the season of success, but must remain satisfied with the season of persistence. Like waiting for an Indian summer that just might never come.

Still, frustration is a fact of life for all of us in one way or another. I've found simple remedies often provide the most relief. Like a walk around the block. If it's a day that's too hot for November, however, a walk may not do the trick. On those days, I might do better to take myself to a movie or even go to the mall and buy myself something special. Sometimes even a bowl of ice cream helps. What I've discovered is that the best way to deal with frustration is give myself a change of scenery, and maybe include a special treat. Sometimes I can write my way out of frustration, creating on paper just the kind of place I'd like to be.

Like weather, frustration isn't something that can always be controlled. It comes and goes of its own accord. What I can do is take care of myself. When I do, I often find that my spirits brighten, usually just in time for a change in the weather.

On a day when frustration strikes, I'll look for new ways to take care of myself.

Exploring Sadness

When was the last time you walked in the rain or mist? How did it make you feel? How did you see the world on such a day? Were you filled with sadness or simply melancholy? Do you think days like this are a necessary part of life? How do you handle such times when they come to you? Are you able to capture a similar mood in your creative efforts? Read "Misty Mornings" and then take your walk, allowing yourself to feel any sadness that arises on such a jaunt.

Misty Mornings

Life, and all that lives, is conceived in the mist and not in the crystal.
—Kahlil Gibran

It's nice to walk in the mist sometimes. The world surrounds you with just a tiny hint of moisture, miniature teardrops from Mother Nature. I always think of misty mornings as sad, but maybe that's just me. The mist tugs at my heartstrings and makes me recall moments I've tucked away in a special memory box and only take out on days such as these. But the memories always seem to have a hint of melancholy about them.

These are sad memories of times gone by, moments that won't ever be captured again but have somehow found a way to imprint themselves on my soul forever. When I consider such moments, I find myself wishing I could go back and recapture that time, change and somehow make the memory different, better. Yet I suppose I have gone back, by simply reliving the memory. The feelings certainly seem as strong today as they were when the event was taking place.

Sometimes I even feel overwhelmed by the feelings—the mist of the morning dots my skin and my clothes and threatens to dampen my spirits more than I care to have them moistened. Melancholy makes me want to curl up beneath the covers with a warm cup of tea nearby. Melancholy is what happens when I realize I can't change the past, I can only accept that what happened is behind me now. When melancholy appears, I take a deep breath and consider that perhaps what I'm being called to do is to remember fully, to grasp those old sensations with my heart open, then carry them back into my world and my work.

Such melancholy, with its memories that last and live on, is what brings soul to my writing. Misty mornings call these moments back to life. If I hold them gently, and cherish them fully, I'll have more to share with others in my words. I can paint pictures that touch the hearts of others just as the mist touches all who choose to walk on such days.

Perhaps I will be sad and melancholy for a time, but as Kahlil Gibran says, "The deeper sorrow cuts into your being, the more joy you can contain." I must hold this sorrow long enough for it to turn to joy, long enough for the mist to fade and the sun to return, long enough for the memories to feed me and help me recapture what I need to bring to my work.

Today, I'll hold my misty memories—I'll turn them to words—until they turn to joy.

Exploring Exhilaration

What exhilarates you? As you walk today, seek out exhilaration. You may see it, or hear it, or feel it. Exhilaration is a different experience for everyone. Consider ways in which you might bring a sense of exhilaration to your writing or other creative endeavor. Write down some of those ideas, then explore them in a stream-of-consciousness essay. Read my essay "Blowing in the Wind" and see how it compares to your own ideas about exhilaration.

Blowing in the Wind

A *little of what you fancy does you good.*
                    —Marie Lloyd

Leaves swirling, some angry, some light and gay like dancers, and some in such a hurry to leave the scene you'd think they were late for somebody's wedding. Trees bending like acrobats, the sound of the branches brushing against each other like creaky overaged musicians. The wind whistles and roars and then catches its breath and does it all over again.

I love the sights and sounds of the wind, but it's the feel of it that really makes me gasp with delight. Today, as I walked, the wind swirled my hair around my head like a dancer's veil; it sucked at my jacket and pants legs like children begging for attention; it caressed my cheek like a lover's breath. And this was just a common wind, a neighborhood wind, not even an exotic wind.

The feel of that wind, however, brought those other winds to my mind. Suddenly, I was transported to another year and another place and the wind in a windy English city was carrying me to see and hear and feel things I'd never experienced before. I remember how I laughed when a little old lady said "it's blowy," wondering if "blowy" was indeed a word. Then, just as quickly, I was whisked away to a beach, walking along the sand with the wind from the waves filling my senses with sea and salt air. I took a long deep breath and even here, in the present moment, could smell the ocean air once more. This moment faded, and I recalled a time on a parapet of a medieval walled city in France, standing with a friend while the wind whipped around us and carried our voices beyond this time and place to futures that would unexpectedly slip into the magic of this special moment.

Moments like this one. Moments filled with wind that bring back the magic of memories. Maybe that's what wind does—it simply blows back memories and swirls them around us until we're laughing with delight over times we never really expected to remember so vividly again. Yet here they are, blowing in the wind. Exhilarating me, filling me up with the champagne of life. Bubbly and bright and leaving me with just a little tingle as I return to my work.

Today, I'll be exhilarated by something magical that I discover as I walk.

Exploring Anger

With fall comes the time when things start to cool off and the memory of summer's heat begins to fade like the last season's bright colors. And there's nothing like a walk to help cool your internal thermometer, especially when anger has it raging out of control. As you walk today, let the cooler air seep into your being and bring calm. Allow your steps to move from hard and heavy to light and brisk. Feel your anger literally melting away into the more relaxed atmosphere of fall. Think of ways to explore these feelings in your creative endeavors. Read "Cooling Off," then write about your own angry experience and what helped you to "cool off."

Cooling Off

Love must be learned and learned again and again; there is no end to it.
—Katherine Anne Porter

I'm steaming over a phone call I just had. I'm a little piqued at something my mother told me last night. I'm not too pleased with my husband's attitude at the moment. I can't focus on my work. I need to cool off. Time for a walk.

Luckily it's a beautiful day and only slightly chilly, not even enough to warrant a coat. I head out at a determined pace, catapulted forward by the force of my anger. Nothing seems to be going right lately. My creative writing sucks, my relationships are all at odds, and work is off schedule.

I can't remember the last time I've felt so full of venom. I could spit fifty feet if given half a chance. But I don't want to spit because it's not lady-like, just like it's not ladylike to be angry. But I am.

My feet hit the pavement hard and heavy, and I notice that my body feels tense and unyielding. I look around and I want to yield. The sun is shining and the day is beautiful. The temperature has dropped to a moderate and comfortable level, reminding me of those California days I love so well. I find myself being grateful for what this day has brought, in spite of myself.

I begin to go back over the things that have been happening in my life, and I realize I haven't been able to take my walk for a few days now. The pressure has been building like beans in the cooker, and today they were just ready to blow, I guess. I think back to the things that are happening—the deadline can be pushed a little, the shopping will all get done, my mother was only trying to be helpful. Normally the things that are bothering me now wouldn't be bothersome at all. When I take the time I need for myself, usually I'm able to meet the world with cooler calm.

Taking some deep breaths, I find my pace is lighter, happier, and I look around, taking a moment to absorb the beauty of this day, this new season. When did my anger go? I wonder. Was it the coolness of the fall air that melted it, or that little bit of gratitude that crept into my heart when I wasn't looking?

All I can think is that now I need to call my mother.

Today I'll let my walk cool off any angry feelings that I'm harboring inside.

Exploring Grandeur

What do you see on your walk today that's grand? What would someone who's never visited your area consider grand about it? Do you find that you tend to overlook those things, having seen them time and time again? What's grand about your life? Do you live "large" or are you settled into a routine that's ordinary and comfortable? Do you have creative dreams that might be considered grand by others, but not by you? Read "The Boulevard of Dreams," then explore what's grand in your own life.

The Boulevard of Dreams

My daughter can spin straw into gold.
—"Rumpelstiltskin"

Sometimes I venture a little farther from home than usual. Not far from my house there's a wide boulevard lined by twenty-year-old pecan trees. In the summer months, full green boughs shade the street like Indian canopies. Now, however, the trees are stripped bare of foliage and the tips of the branches reach across the street to touch like lovers' hands. No matter what the season, whenever I walk or drive that way I always feel I'm heading somewhere important. It's my personal boulevard of dreams with something grand waiting at the end.

I've seen such avenues in movies—where horse-driven carriages carry richly dressed occupants to exquisite gardens and a grand palace still hidden beyond the tree-lined road. I'm amazed that I have such an avenue to travel every day. I'm delighted that such a grand boulevard leads to my home. What dreams and magic await me at the end is purely up to me.

I think I also forget that there's nothing wrong with having grand dreams waiting for you at the end of the boulevard: the best-selling novel, the award-winning screenplay, the new life in a place where everyone says it's too expensive to live. Sometimes we let the attitudes of others pull us away from those dreams of greatness. But holding on and pursuing those dreams gives our lives purpose.

As I stroll up the street, I realize that sometimes I let the grandness of my life slip away from me. I forget the simple things that a newcomer might find incredible—this majestic tree-lined street, the virgin prairie land with its brilliant spring wildflowers a short distance from my house, the old turreted church around the corner. Small grandnesses, perhaps, but noteworthy all the same.

The journey toward our dreams may be long, and it's important to enjoy the process, to take note of the tree-lined boulevard as we go. We need to practice, as Sarah Ban Breathnach tells us in *Simple Abundance*, "the habit of being—the exultation in the present moment."

But I'm also determined to remember that I, too, can spin gold out of straw by remembering, as metaphysician and author Joseph Murphy writes, "There is a gold mine within you from which you can extract everything you need to live life gloriously, joyously, and abundantly."

Today I'll remember to look for the grandness in the ordinary.

Exploring Pruning

Fall is a time to prune the trees. Are there things that need to be pruned in your life? What are they? What purpose does pruning serve? Have you used this in the past to change a growth pattern? How did it work? What changes do you see in trees and shrubs when they're pruned? Do you take time to prune your creative work? Read "Trimming Time" and then consider how you might get to work doing some pruning of your own.

Trimming Time

Often while you are doing writing practice you have no idea whether you have written anything good or not.
—Natalie Goldberg

Fall has wound down to winter, and the trees are stripped bare. This is the time when people begin to think about pruning their trees. Sometimes I see them, standing in their front yards, cradling their chins, staring up at the broad limbs, considering how best to plan for the growth of the coming year. Do I want shade in this part of the yard? How much must I cut to make sure those branches aren't scraping the roof like they did last summer? If I cut as much as I like, will the tree's growth be stunted?

Personally, I hate to see the actual trimming. Men or women, attached to ladders and lines, wielding saws, hacking at the tree, inflicting what seem to be mortal wounds. After they've finished their work, the tree stands like a permanently maimed soldier—limbs amputated, left with only cruel memories of a previous glory. It's hard to see them so violated, and I inadvertently turn my eyes away, shielding myself from the pain they will rest in for the remainder of the season.

But then, miraculously, when the season turns, they do as well. Tree or shrub, each seems to return to a fuller bloom than I would have imagined possible. It's as if they needed the pruning to force them into a time of rest, and once rested, they're able to return with a vengeance.

I would do well to do my own pruning each winter. What better time to cut back, slow down, pull into myself and prepare for awakening in the spring. I suspect all people, but creative ones in particular, need this time to rest and regroup. Since we're constantly putting so much out, digging deep into ourselves to find the words and ideas with which to flower our work, it stands to reason that a season of sleep would be needed. Downtime might include not creating for a time—be you a writer, artist, or carpenter. It might be doing something fun and different, taking your mind and body to some totally new experience.

At first we may feel bare, as if we've been stripped of the very things that give us life, and we'll never blossom again. But somehow we do; somehow the time of rest always results in enhanced creativity and better work. Trimming back provides the vitality we need to stay on a path that requires at the very least a vast amount of persistence.

Now as I walk, I find I can face the starkness of a tree that's been recently trimmed. Now, I know the trimming isn't an indication of what's been lost, but a message about what's to come.

Today, I'll seek to trim back and prepare for the coming spring of my creative work.

Exploring the Fullness of Fall

Why does fall make us think of abundance? What is it about the crisp cooler days that makes us feel full of gratitude that spills over into everything we do? Do you feel abundance with regard to your creativity? In what way? Read "Hidden in the Leaves" and, as you walk today, look for subtle and obvious examples of abundance, then consider how you might bring some of that abundance home with you.

Hidden in the Leaves

Expect nothing. Live frugally on surprise.
—Alice Walker

Fall is winding down, and its burnt-orange colors have changed to a crisp definite brown. Most of the leaves have fallen and it's time for me and my neighbors to think about getting out our rakes and plastic bags. Some of the more ambitious folks already have growing piles decorating their yards.

I don't know why, but piles of leaves just seem to bring out my child-like self, and suddenly I feel mischievous. I have to admit I've been known to kick at the edges of these piles if they happen to be in my path. It's just too good an opportunity to pass up. In my mind, I'm already diving into that ocean of leaves like a kid on the first day of summer; it wouldn't take long to undo someone's long afternoon of work. Luckily, I haven't actually stooped to such extremes—still I can't say I wouldn't love to give it a go!

Why do piles of leaves draw me so? I wondered as I walked recently. What secret lies hidden in the middle of those remnants of the season? Maybe it's knowing that no matter how many times I flatten those leaves, there's always going to be another pile, another sign of the abundance the universe offers.

All those leaves remind me that there's creative abundance as well. I can write and write, and no matter how many words I put on paper, how many ideas I come up with, there's always going to be another batch of them ready to be gathered up and written. The universe manufactures new ideas like leaves on a tree—no stinginess in either category.

Fall is a time when people like to think about harvest, to remember with gratitude all they've been given. Sometimes when I know I've got to rake my own front yard, all I can think is "all those leaves." But there they are, ready to bring out my forgotten playfulness, ready to remind me not only of the abundance of ideas they might represent, but the abundance of memories as well.

Today, I may just take a dive into a pile of leaves, to help me remember the abundance of the universe.

The Wonders of Walking

Winter Explorations

Winter. Time for stillness and reflection. The world has stilled itself and given you a chance to notice how even nature has to rest and replenish. Winter brings with it the perfect opportunity to look back on the accomplishments of the preceding year. What inspired you in the spring? Where did you place your focus during the summer months? Did you follow through with discipline in the fall? What have you achieved during the past year that has changed or enhanced your life? During this season, give yourself a chance to revel in your successes and reconsider endeavors that may have seemed less than successful.

Winter also provides a wonderful time for deciding where you want to head in the upcoming year. During this silent season, perfect for days indoors with tea and books, create a place to listen to your inner voice and determine what it's asking from you for the days ahead. What is winter calling you to reconsider? Perhaps you've been reluctant to explore certain possibilities for your life; maybe your focus has been scattered or dim, or maybe overload has left you feeling drained and unfulfilled. If necessary, you can use winter's downtime for a complete personal overhaul!

Allow your journey to be slowed during the days ahead. Remind yourself that this is the circle of life—the winter rest—that gives every living thing the opportunity for renewal in the spring. You, too, are a part of the circle. Give your heart to winter, and you will find your soul revived come spring.

Exploring Ebb and Flow

How do you feel about gray days? Do they motivate you to create or make you want to curl up with tea and a good book? Are you able to go with the flow of winter's gray days, or are you impatient for the bleak skies to pass and return to blue again? What in particular do you see as you walk today that speaks of the ebb and flow of life? How do you deal with changes in your life? How do gray days affect your creativity? Read "Gray Days" then reflect on ways you're affected by this season's cloudy skies.

Gray Days

Light tomorrow with today.

—Elizabeth Barrett Browning

Gray days are those days that you just can't seem to motivate yourself to get out of the house. The sky is dreary, it's cold, and you're just not up to the usual walking routine. Gray days are the days when you want to forget how good walking is for you, and remain nice and warm in your snuggly cocoon until spring arrives. I know all about gray days—I'm having one today.

Sometimes the best thing to do on a gray day is to give in to it. Let yourself have that time at home, sitting by the fire, reading a good book, and sipping a hot cup of tea. Sometimes that's exactly what you need to be doing! It's good to listen to that friend inside who's telling you to take it easy. But a trick I've used when that friend starts nagging that exercise is good for me is to tell myself I'll just take a little walk. I'll walk slow and enjoy the day instead of trying to push myself into the fat-burning zone. Once I'm going, I usually end up wanting to combine my stroll with a little aerobic walking as well. And suddenly I'm feeling better about myself. It doesn't matter if the day is gray or blue or a funny shade of orange—I'm out, and I'm enjoying it.

Some days, though, I don't need to use my little trick. Some days, a gray day is just what I need. Gray days are days when the world is resting, when the curtains are pulled over the sun so we'll know we need to slow down and take a breath. As I walk on days when the sky is overcast, I like to think about changes—in the seasons, in the world, in my own life. I am reminded that nothing ever stays the same. No matter what my mood, my situation, my plans, change is as inevitable—and as unpredictable—as the weather. Learning to accept life's ebbing and flowing has been one of my greatest personal challenges. Moments still arise when I struggle against this natural course, but they are fewer and further between than they once were. The solitude of my daily walks has provided a source of calm and inspiration to me as I've traveled this inner path, and I believe the days when the sky has been cloudy and a bit ominous are when I've experienced the most valuable insight.

Today, gray skies will not dissuade me from remembering that more often than not, shadows curtain light.

Exploring Special Places

Do certain types of days call to mind certain places for you? Do you have a secret or special place where you always feel safe and at home? Where is that place and what circumstances in your daily life recall it for you? Are there places you can walk to recapture a sense of that place? What are they like? Do you feel you are most creative in your special place? In what ways does your creativity express itself when you are there? Can you bring that home with you? Read "California Blue," then write about your own special place.

California Blue

When you have fulfilled yourself, you can give out of abundance.
—Stephen C. Paul

It's a crisp cool winter day and the sky is a deeper shade of blue than I've seen it in some time. On days when the sky is blue like this, it doesn't matter if it's cold or warm, if the wind's racing around you like a toddler begging for a spin in the air; I always recall the way I felt when I spent the summer in California. My heart just bursts with this energy that seems to come from nowhere and lifts me up on wings of light.

California—especially the Los Angeles area—is my special place. In *The Education of Little Tree* the boy talks about a secret place of his own, remarking "when I saw it, I knew it was my secret place, so I went there a whole lot." His was a small place on the side of a mountain; mine was an entire city, and a big one at that. No matter: your heart doesn't ask where you want your special place to be—it just knows when you're there.

In that place, you imagine that anything you want to do, you can do. You have the energy, the intelligence, and the confidence to make your dreams a reality in that place. It's magic. Life is better than ordinary there. Maybe it's in the stars, as I once had an astrologer tell me, or maybe it's a past-life thing, when we long to return to something we've known before. Maybe it's because your special place is where everything you love—be it people, place, or philosophy—comes together in just the right way.

I only know that today, walking along the streets of my neighborhood with the sun warming my face and the blue up above, I was transported to that place for a short while. As I walked, I called to mind the images I'd tucked neatly away and I let them remind me that no matter where I am, or what I'm doing, or even how badly I'm feeling, that place is always there, waiting for my return. Better yet, I can even carry it home with me, and allow those memories to bring that sense of possibility into whatever work I'm doing, however trivial my routine may have become.

Little Tree's grandma told him that your special place is where you go to understand the difference between body-mind and spirit-mind, and in that place, you come to better understand spirit-mind as you watch the seasons pass by. Walking in general helps my spirit-mind watch and understand, but walking in my special place, or on a day that brings to mind that place, is a joy.

Today I'll let thoughts of my special place infuse my life and fill me with joy and vitality.

Exploring Individuality

Listen for the songs of wind chimes while you're walking. What are they singing about as they tinkle in the breeze? Do you like the sound or does it bother you? Why? What are some different types of chimes? Can you hear the individual sound of each chime? How might you describe the different sounds? How would you write your own "wind chime song"? In what ways do you bring individuality into your creative work? What about your work is uniquely you? Now read "The Music of the Chimes."

The Music of the Chimes

Without music, life would be a mistake.
—Friedrich Nietzsche

Like walking, music can be a natural place to turn when seeking creative release. How many artists have you read or heard about who insist on having background music while working? Don't we all have specific kinds of music that we turn to for inspiration or relaxation or even stimulation? Music certainly soothes and inspires me while I'm in the creative process; in fact, I usually have a favorite CD playing while I work. Some of my favorite mood music is the lovely piano solos and New Age keyboards, but there's nothing like a good dose of rock and roll to get me moving when I need a little extra push.

On my walk today, however, I discovered a new kind of music, and as

I write this essay, I'm listening to strains of it playing outside my window. Wind chime music is a little like a cross between experimental jazz and *Tubular Bells* (remember the music that became a hit after the release of the *The Exorcist*?). Wind chimes are all over the place; they're wind made audible, and their song is different on any given day.

Although I heard several different tonalities as I walked today—from the deep vibrant music of the larger, heavier chimes to the delicate tinkles of tiny tubes—my favorite are the midsized carillons, the well-rounded harmonies that speak to me of the need for balance, a necessary return to one's center.

Chimes provide a great example for living one's life. Chimes work in unity; each part of the song depends on the other parts, and the center is what makes the best music. Some chimes hang suspended from a horizontal bar; these are less likely to make music unless a pretty heavy wind comes up. The rest of the time, they're suspended in isolation from each other, waiting for that wind that will unite them in song. But the chimes that make the best music are those with a center, that slender thread that holds the bar or flat metal circle that each tube must strike to play its note. These chimes only need a slight breeze to send them swaying and playing against their core, creating a song unlike any other.

We have the potential to turn our life and work into a unique song. To do so, however, we have to return to that center, not just with our ego or our talent or our spirituality or our intellect, but with all aspects of ourselves. When we find that core, we're just like the wind chime—being blown about only provides the world with a better melody.

Today, I'll listen to the notes playing inside of me and begin to create my own unique song.

Exploring Connections

When winter comes and the trees are bare, what do they bring to your mind as you walk? In their long slender boughs reaching skyward, do you see signs of hope or despair? What connections do they seem to be reaching toward? How do you find connections in your creativity? Is connection important to you? Read "Spidery Webs" and then explore the need for connection in your life.

Spidery Webs

> *I think that wherever your journey takes you, there are new gods [and goddesses] waiting there, with divine patience, and laughter.*
> —Susan M. Watkins

When the trees are finally bare and their stark skinny limbs reach outward, seeming to seek connection with each other against the sky, I'm often reminded of those spidery webs one sees in summer. The spider spins and links those lines of slender thread, providing a safe haven for itself and its offspring, as well as a source of sustenance. Squinting against bright light, I study those webs against the sky, wondering about the implications of those connections, which sometimes seem so frail and tenuous, as if the slightest breeze could break them completely, leaving each tree alone and isolated in the winter chill.

Walking beneath these silent voices of nature, tall and austere in the cold, I realize that I, too, often stand alone. As an artist, I work from a place of solitude and isolation, alone in a world that often turns a cold shoulder to such creators. Often, artists work in isolation, often by choice, as the voices of our muses seem to demand silence in order to be heard. But silence and solitude can become trying—people need connection, and sharing the life force of others rounds out a daily routine. It's important that I remember it's sometimes necessary to extend my own fragile arms, to seek others who've chosen this same way of life. When I find these connections, I too am provided with a sheltering cocoon and sustenance. I too am supported by slender threads.

Even now, as I walk in the chill of this season, those webs against the sky remind me that we must all reach out and seek the connections that allow us to remember we aren't alone. I believe each of us has an obligation to follow the path of our heart—be that the path of an artist, an engineer, or a homemaker. Sometimes we'll walk the path alone and in silence, but there will also be times to walk with others, to share our time and our talents.

I stop for a moment, and put my face against the cold hard bark of one particular tree, one that seems to stand taller, stronger than the others, one whose arms seek to reach farther and grasp tighter. This is the kind of tree I want to be. I want to be a tree who doesn't wait for others to reach out, but who reaches out itself, spinning the web, offering support to those who may not be strong enough to reach for it. I want to be the person who calls first, to see if the friend is lonely; to bring together her neighbors to share a meal and community—the one who takes time to ask and listen. I want those same things to come back full strength to me, when it's my turn.

Offering support is necessary not only in art, but in life. The message that reaches me today is that I need to find ways to reach for other hands, offering them my strength and my shelter in whatever ways I can.

Today, I open my heart to others, offering connection and shelter.

Exploring Focus

Do you know where life is taking you, or do you just seem to float with the tide? Are you able to maintain focus in your work, or do you constantly struggle against moving off track? Does walking help you focus? If so, in what ways? Why do you think it's important to stay focused? Are there times when it's better just to let yourself float? Read "A Dog's Life," then consider your own attitudes about focus.

A Dog's Life

My favorite thing is to go where I've never been.
                                    —Diane Arbus

Have you ever paid much attention to dogs when you're walking? Ideally, dogs should be on a leash or in someone's fenced yard. However, around my neighborhood, I frequently see dogs that aren't where they're supposed to be.

Mostly, dogs know where they're going. Or at least they seem to . . . The big reddish-brown Lab I saw last week certainly appeared to have a specific destination in mind. This dog was in a pretty big hurry, and he passed me on the sidewalk without even a backward sniff. He did, however, stop to smell the fire hydrant at the corner and mark the spot as his territory.

Since he turned the same corner I was about to turn, I got to watch this fellow for a while longer, sniffing under bushes and flowerbeds, pausing from time to time to give a passing tree a quick squirt. But obviously, he had a mission, and he kept moving forward.

I started thinking that I might be a better writer if I worked with the focus of a dog. For one thing, that dog just kept moving—oh, he paused from time to time to check out something that caught his interest, but not for one second did he let whatever caught his fancy deter him from his original goal, whatever that was. People mark territory, too, in their own way. Certain places along the way, like certain completed works or moments in our lives, are worth marking. They make a particular impression and they're important, and as a result we should return to them from time to time to remind ourselves who we are, where we've been, and what matters. But if we get hung up in one particular spot, we'll never make it to our destination. Achieving our goals—whatever they may be—is the result of movement rather than resting or waiting in any one place.

Dogs have the right attitude, too. If another dog or a cat or a person indicates the dog isn't wanted, what does the dog do? It just moves on. No hesitation, no whining, no resistance. Somehow, the dog recognizes there'll be other opportunities.

Dogs don't make a big deal of things, but the one I met today had some big things to say in a not so big way. But that's the way it usually goes, isn't it?

Today, I'll maintain the focus of a dog and the attitude as well.

Exploring Detail

Have you noticed how occasionally the brisk cold of winter brings things into better focus than the warm blurring of summer days? The lines of the trees, the outlines of houses against a sharp blue sky, the tiny bare branches of shrubs and flowers become crisp and clear in the heart of winter. What do you see as you walk today? Note the details and then read "Delighting in the Details" and see what you can bring home to incorporate into your creative work

Delighting in the Details

The frost never paints my windows twice alike.
—Lydia Maria Child

Writers have to pay attention to details. They tell us that in all the writing classes, but when you're sitting in front of a keyboard surrounded by nothing that has anything to do with whatever subject you're writing about, it's not that easy. That's why I like to make notes when I walk—especially in the winter. For some reason, I see things more clearly during this season. Spring and summer flow through me like a glass of fine wine—I feel a little intoxicated by all the bright colors and the sweet scents and the fullness in the air. Fall makes me want to work, to get moving and ready, rather than slowing down and paying attention.

In winter, I move more slowly, my feet carrying me along the way at a brisk enough pace, but my inner self is somehow more open and obser-vant. Maybe it's because the world has suddenly been stripped bare, and now I can see what's beneath the veil of green and the masks of bright color.

I'm not sure why they say "the devil's in the details"—I find the details a delight, even in a season when the predominant colors are gray and brown. Otherwise, I might never have noticed that knothole twisted into the shape of a figure eight in the tree on the corner, or the shrub in my neighbor's yard that looks like a frantic woman tearing out what's left of her summer hair with twenty thin brown arms, or the pale buttercup yellow of the house sitting half a mile away, never visible through the foliage of the trees.

I make note of all these amazing little details. These are the elements I'll take home with me, and use them to color my writing in times and seasons when details don't come quite so easily. I fill up pages, looking for more detail as I write. How can I describe the buttercup yellow house so that it becomes clearer to my reader? What would the knothole in the tree remind them of? Why is that frantic woman tearing out her hair? Exploring the details is a never-ending source of surprise. And everyone loves to be surprised!

Today, I'll open my eyes, my heart, and my mind to the details exposed by winter.

Exploring Patterns

Have you ever walked a labyrinth? Is there anywhere in your area you might go to have this experience? Have you ever tried to create a pattern in your daily walking? What are some of the benefits of patterned walks? Do you find pleasure or frustration in having to walk in a structured way? Read "Walking the Maze" and reflect on any patterned walking you may have done. If you haven't walked a maze, you may want to explore this type of walking.

Walking the Maze

Sometimes a person has to go back, really back—to have a sense, an understanding of all that's gone to make them—before they can go forward.
—Paule Marshall

Last winter I had an opportunity to take a labyrinth walk. A labyrinth is a pattern that's been laid out on the floor or ground, and you follow its circular path from a starting point to a finishing point. I imagine this kind of walk would have been wonderful in ancient times, walking the revolutions of a hill through a white misty fog.

When I walked my first labyrinth—the only one to date!—I spent some time sitting beforehand, focusing on my feelings and getting centered. In this case, the maze was patterned on material and spread on the floor. It was smaller than I expected, so it got a bit tricky when I came upon other people walking in the opposite direction. The idea of the labyrinth is to follow the pattern into its center; there you can pray or meditate or whatever you choose until you're ready to start out again. On the outward path, if you meet other people going toward the center, either you or they must step aside to let the other pass. I thought it would be more complicated and disturbing than it actually was to have other people on the labyrinth. But everyone on the labyrinth is on their own path, even though in reality the path is the same. While walking, you become so focused on your own journey that you really aren't thinking about what anyone else is doing. The best thing to do during an encounter is simply to bless that passing and move on.

What I found most amazing (no pun intended!) about the walk was that going toward the center felt confusing and uncertain. Was I supposed to take that turn or go straight? When I stepped aside for a moment, did I get turned around as I started forward again? Didn't I already walk this revolution? I was never quite sure I was going the right way.

Once in the center, however, I felt more focused; then, as I began my way out, the path seemed easier to follow, more direct. Is it possible that since I'd already traveled the road once, I felt more confident it would lead me out? Perhaps so, but what I decided was that it's all simply a metaphor for the way we walk the paths of our lives. All walks are patterned walks, to some extent, and the patterns eventually lead us exactly where we need to be. We may not see the pattern at first, and we may feel confused and uncertain, but if we keep moving, eventually we will begin to understand and to feel more secure about our journey.

Now, though I enjoy varying my walks from time to time, I always try to see their patterns, the messages and blessings along the way.

Today, I'll look for ways to discover how the patterns in my walk match the patterns in my life.

Exploring Possibility

Are you open to possibilities and new opportunities? In what ways do you create an open space within for new experiences? If you are not open to possibility, why? How do you think you could change this? As you explore this idea on a winter walk, what do you see that reminds you of the importance of being open to everything—new ideas, new horizons, new creations? Read "The Purity of Snow" and then write your own reflections about the development of an open attitude in your life.

The Purity of Snow

It's never too late to be what you might have been.
—George Eliot

In my part of the country, we don't get a whole lot of snow. A friend of mine has a small house in Colorado, though, and I'm fortunate enough to be able to visit this mountain area and have the experience of pure white snow. Nothing awakens my sense of possibility than a field of snow. A white pure mountainside covered with a fresh coat of snow reminds me of a blank page, waiting to be filled with new words, new thoughts and ideas.

Sometimes, the blank page can be frightening. Knowing that it's time to fill the space with new experiences, I may hold back. In writing, I may experience a block. In life, I may refuse to take risks, to move in a direction I know I need to go.

I've felt this reluctance often in my own life. Most recently it's been literally making a move, leaving a home and life to which I've grown accustomed even though I know in my heart it's time to move on. I don't want to walk on the snow; I want to keep its purity intact forever. No such luck, I'm afraid. The snow will melt, life will move on, and the possibilities will become regrets for what could have been.

When I see the snow beginning to melt a couple of days later, I also notice that it's dotted with footprints—animals have walked there, and perhaps even a person or two. I realize that I, too, must walk in the snow. I must open myself to the possibilities of the fresh page when I begin a new writing project, to the opportunities that a new day brings to make a mark.

It's wonderful to stay with a moment of pure white snow, to enjoy that moment to its fullest. But as the moment moves forward, so must I.

Today, I open myself to the possibilities that a new day brings.

Exploring Passion

When was the last time you felt passion in your life? Was it for your work or perhaps a new hobby? Relationships aren't the only way to experience passion. How long has it been since you felt an internal heat, the excitement of beginning something new? As you brace yourself for a cold winter walk today, consider the heat passion brings to your life and think about ways to thaw the cold you may have allowed to grow inside. Read "Bonfire Blazes" and write about what heats your own soul.

Bonfire Blazes

Within your heart, keep one still secret spot where dreams may go.

—Louise Driscoll

Deep in the midst of an arctic freeze both inside and out, I'm not feeling much like walking today. Bundled up like a baby in a snowsuit, I'm bracing myself against the cold, as I'm determined to make my daily trek around the neighborhood despite the icicles hanging outside the front door. Once moving, it's not so bad, and I begin to comfort myself with the idea of a nice warm fire once I'm back at home. I don't have a fireplace so my gas logs will have to do the trick.

Thinking about fire makes me long for those youthful days of passionate kisses around a bonfire. There's nothing like cuddling up with someone when you're experiencing the first throes of passion, the heat of your bodies blended with the fire's warm glow. It's magic. It warms me just to remember. What makes me shiver a little, however, is the thought of just how long it's been since I had a firsthand experience of passion.

Suddenly, however, I recall a day a few weeks ago when the sun was shining and the blue sky reminded me of days spent on the beach last summer. I remember how I felt that warm, tingly sensation of passion surging through my body and enveloping me with the pleasure of a moment that wasn't this moment, yet had become a part of it all the same. Kind of like a moment ago, when I was remembering the bonfire and that warm wonderful kiss of some boy whose name I can't even recall. A moment gone forever, yet brought back in the blink of an instant.

I begin to think about other passionate moments—working on a movie on a hot summer day, walking in England along the coastal path where my first novel was set, having afternoon tea in a spectacular garden with a dear friend, playing with a child in a blanket fort. I find myself warmed by these memories. I'm so warmed, I find myself shedding an outer layer of clothing, enjoying the briskness of the day where moments before I'd felt only its chill.

I'm amazed at the power of these moments to warm my heart, to take me back to times of passion and allow that passion to live in me once again, making this moment a passionate one as well. I pick up the pace, eager to get back to my home and my little gas logs, to make a cup of tea and allow this day's passion to wash over and infuse me with heat I hadn't realized was there.

Passion often comes unexpectedly. Today, I'll find it where I least expected it.

Exploring Unity

An icy day isn't always a good day for a walk. However, if the ice is melting and the sun is shining and your feet are itching for your daily stroll, pay attention to the signs of unity offered by the melting ice. Consider how water goes to rain goes to snow goes to water. How are other things in our lives so united? Do you see other signs of this unity as you walk? Where is the unity in your creative efforts? Read "Ice Storms" and then write some of your own thoughts about unity.

Ice Storms

The world is round and the place which may seem like the end may also be only the beginning.

—Ivy Baker Priest

The water goes drip, drip, drip down the slender line of the icicle, melting into puddles on the ground. Puddles I pass, puddles I step in, puddles that seep into the earth and feed the sleeping plants. What doesn't go to puddles is absorbed into the air, eventually coming back to me as rain, or snow, or sleet, or maybe another ice storm. As I walk today, I think about the unity of the world—one thing always leading to another, all things connected in some often obscure way.

Yesterday, it was interesting to watch people reacting to the ice that was headed our way. Most people wanted to hurry home to avoid traffic and danger on the road. Some were upset because poor street conditions were affecting their plans for the evening. Others were adamant that roads and weather wouldn't be as bad as the meteorologists were predicting. Everyone had their own opinion, but the consensus seemed to be that no one was happy about the approaching storm.

Today, however, the value of this winter storm seems perfectly clear. Not only do icy roads slow people down—and during this season of hustle and bustle who doesn't need to be slowed down?—the water replenishes the plants and trees after the drought of the past summer. The ice sparkles in the sunlight, making me feel as if I'm walking in a jewel box, catching glimpses of riches that haven't cost me a cent. The world is brighter and happier for all the "badness" of the weather.

Listening to the steady drops of water falling from trees and the eaves of houses as I pass, I'm delighted with a song that can only be sung during the winter. The delicate gurgle of water reminds me of the circle and unity of nature, how everything has its time and purpose.

I notice as I round the corner toward home that the clouds are hanging heavy, perhaps boding another evening storm, another round of icy cold for the night. I'm thankful for the fire that waits for me, the warmth of my room with a cup of tea and a good book, perhaps an afternoon nap. But I'm also thankful for the cold and the wet and the ice. And I hope that tomorrow there may be another symphony of water and another stroll around the jewel box.

I am united with all that is and was and ever will be.

Exploring Rhythms

Do you pay attention to the rhythms in your life? When you're walking, do you find yourself moving in a slow steady rhythm, or do you have a brisk rapid pace? Does the pace of your walk carry over into your daily routines? In what ways? Notice the movement of your body as you walk today, then see if you find that same pace carrying over into your work. Read "The Magic of Movement" and then explore your own thoughts about movement and rhythm.

The Magic of Movement

The rhythm of walking generates a rhythm of thinking.
—Rebecca Solnit

Walking provides me with much more than just exercise. I suspect this may be true for other creative types as well, and if you haven't discovered the side benefits of walking, you might want to give it a go. Sometimes I forget how important walking is to me until I'm doing it and experiencing some kind of breakthrough. Sometimes this has to do with a relationship, sometimes a problem with my work, and sometimes, the best of times, it's about my writing.

As I've mentioned more than once, sometimes it's a struggle for me to hit the road. Especially on days when it's cold or gray, or I'm just not in the mood. Today, in the heart of winter and the busiest time of year in my work as a textbook editor, I didn't want to go out. Not to mention that I've been trying to put the finishing touches on this book of walking meditations, and I need to be at my desk. But then I hit that brick wall where the creativity wouldn't flow and the stiff muscle in my neck wouldn't release and the only thing for it was to take a walk.

So I'm walking my usual route, wondering what in the world I'm going to write about, and suddenly I realize I'm in the groove. I'm feeling good and my heart's beating fast enough to give me an extra surge of warming energy—it's almost like I'm dancing to the flow of life. Just moving right along with it, in perfect step with the tempo of the day. Everything feels right.

That's what walking does for me. If I get up and go with it, everything falls into place. The neck muscles relax and are ready for another round at the desk; the energy pumps me up for all I need to accomplish, today and in the days ahead. And the beauty of it is, I know I won't just feel it today, I'll feel it every day that I allow myself this simple pleasure. Walking resets my rhythm.

When I round the corner and see my house just ahead, I'm excited, because I know I can carry this rhythm back inside with me and be ready for whatever the day might bring. Sun, rain, cold, or heat: it really doesn't matter—there's always something waiting for me on the walk.

Today I'll let the magic of movement restore rhythm to my life.

Exploring Hope

What evidence of hope do you see as you walk during the holiday season? How do you feel during the holidays? Are you filled with hope, or simply stressed out about everything that needs to be done? Do the festive displays of the season bring hopeful thoughts to your heart? What are they? What evidence of such hope do you see in others during the season? Consider what hopes you have for your life as you walk today. Read "Love and Miracles," then write about your own hopes for this season and beyond.

Love and Miracles

> *There are two ways of spreading light: to be the candle or the mirror that reflects it.*
>
> —Edith Wharton

Hope fills the air like cinnamon potpourri—it's the holiday season! Why does this season, more than any other, make us believe in love and miracles? Where does that hope come from that suddenly permeates our hearts and lives and makes us believe anything and everything is possible? Isn't that the reason we all smile a little brighter and feel a little kinder during this season?

As I walk, I see houses beaming with the same hope I'm feeling. Decked out in their seasonal finery, garlands of green, lights twinkling like tiny fairies come to life, bows of bright red, and candy cane decorations tempting us with sweet promises—the homes I pass remind me that something important is on the horizon. Something wonderful is about to happen!

The faithful among us might say that something is the birth of a baby in a manger, and perhaps that's as good a way to look at it as any. It's the end of the year, and what's to come is a clean slate, a new year to fill any way we choose. We can fill it with love and miracles, shaped by our own hearts and hands. We can fill it with our talents and our gifts.

As I make my way down the same streets I've walked so often over the past year, my mind turns back to days when I haven't been so hopeful, when I haven't believed in miracles or loved myself and others in ways that might have benefited us both. I realize it's not easy to keep the holiday spirit alive throughout the year, but if we could, we might find the world a nicer place to live.

What's helped most to keep me balanced and happy over the past year are the walks I've taken, the miracles I've found along ordinary paths. The glow of this holiday season seems merely a culmination of spring's bloom, summer's warmth, fall's bounty, and winter's exposed delights. I find myself making a resolution to always carry in my own heart the spark of hope I found in all those seasons. Maybe that spark will catch and light the fires of others.

I breathe deeply, inhaling the smell of fires on the hearth, fires that might be carrying my spark of hope to the families living inside those houses, making them want to carry their own sparks back out into the world. Suddenly I remember a line: "Hope springs eternal!"—not just in spring, but year-round.

Today I'll let a spark of hope light my heart and then spread to others in my life.

Printed in the United States
123103LV00001B/34-39/A